D0933833

DEMCO

Portrait of a Decade

The 1970s

ELIZABETH CAMPLING

B.T. Batsford Ltd, London

Contents

The original idea for the Portrait of a Decade series was conceived by Trevor Fisher.

Typeset by Tek-Art Ltd Kent
and printed and bound
in Great Britain by
The Bath Press, Bath
for the publishers
B.T. Batsford Ltd
4 Fitzhardinge Street
London W1H 0AH

ISBN 0 7134 5988 3

Frontispiece: feminists disrupt the 1970 Miss World Contest at the Albert Hall in London.

Introduction

Unlike other decades, no one has yet succeeded in putting a label on the 1970s. For many who were young and idealistic in the 1960s it was a grey and dreary end to an age of dreams and excitement. For others, who disapproved of the turmoil of the sixties, the seventies were a period when political and cultural extremism reached a climax before the world came to its senses in the sober and hard-headed 1980s. But for those who came of age in the decade the picture is often quite different. For them the 1970s were a time of exciting cultural and social experiment and change, although it is often debatable just how deep or long-lasting those changes were. How historians of the future will judge the 1970s is still far from clear. That is part of the decade's fascination.

A violent decade

During the early years of the decade the rebellious spirit of the sixties was still very much alive. In the United States student rebellion and anti-war agitation rose to new heights. Following the example of American Blacks, underprivileged groups like women and gays made vigorous and sometimes violent demands that society recognize their rights. The same was true of national minorities all over the world, among them Palestinians, French Canadians, Native Americans and Northern Irish Catholics. Time after time the headlines were grabbed by acts of terrorism. Angry and disaffected groups kidnapped individuals and hijacked planes in order to blackmail governments and draw attention to their plight. In Italy and Germany young rebels took their fight against conventional society on to the streets in waves of urban terrorism.

There were many unfinished quarrels left over from the sixties. The Vietnam War was still going on and its repercussions were to be felt throughout the decade. Palestinian Arabs, who lost their lands to Israel in the wars of 1948 and 1967, waited in their refugee camps for a fourth Arab-Israeli War to restore them to their homes. Since 1968 tensions had run high in Northern Ireland, where the Protestant majority rejected the demands of their Catholic neighbours for political and economic equality. The Irish Republican Army (IRA), whose aim was a united Ireland and a total British withdrawal, saw a golden opportunity to make converts. In 1969 British troops had been sent in to keep the peace between the warring communities.

In 1970 there was still no settlement in sight in Southern Rhodesia (Zimbabwe), whose all-white government had declared an illegal unilateral independence (UDI) from Britain in 1965 rather than allow free elections and black majority rule. In 1972 black nationalists were to begin a guerilla war that was to last almost to the end of the seventies.

A changing world

The 1970s produced their own crop of changes to the political map of the world. Democracy returned to Spain and Portugal after decades of dictatorship. China came out of isolation and repaired her relations with the

A changing world – Iran after the Shah. An armed Muslim clergyman marches with the army.

Introduction

United States. Israel and Egypt made peace, and West Germany was reconciled with her Eastern neighbours almost 30 years after the end of the Second World War. The Shah of Iran was ousted and the Persian Gulf became a new world 'hot spot'. In the closing days of 1979, the Russians shocked world opinion by invading Afghanistan. An American President – Nixon – resigned in disgrace.

The crisis of the West

In the middle years of the decade, the confidence of the industrialized nations was shaken to its foundations by the Arab oil embargo of 1973-4 and the great recession that followed. Almost overnight, the unthinking assumption that economic growth and rising living standards would go on indefinitely was shattered. As never before, people became aware that the earth's resources were not unlimited and might one day – maybe not too far in the future – run out. The era when the industrialized nations dominated the world seemed to be drawing to a close. This loss of confidence in the West was to have serious political repercussions on the rest of the decade.

Doubts about technology

The seventies produced few outstanding technological breakthroughs, but earlier inventions like the microprocessor and supersonic aircraft came of age and changed the way people lived. At the same time, technological progress was no longer accepted as being automatically good. Frightening evidence of large-scale pollution and a series of industrial accidents brought home the lesson that unchecked technology could have catastrophic human and environmental side effects. Words like 'ecology' and 'conservation' became part of the every-day vocabulary. The same caution was shown towards medical advances. In spite of dramatic breakthroughs like the birth of the first test tube baby, people became more aware that science had its limits. Man was not, and maybe never could be, all-knowing and all-powerful. Caring for one's own body through a healthier lifestyle became a seventies' cult.

Culture clash

The 1960s had seen that great relaxation in standards of social and sexual behaviour, that became known as the permissive society. By the 1970s it was clear that many changes had come to stay and were accepted across society, and not only by the young. In matters like pre-marital sex, single parenthood or divorce there would be no turning the clock back to the more rigid norms of the 1950s. During the 1960s the popular arts like pop music and films had become important mediums of artistic expression and social comment, which often tried to challenge or shock society out of its complacency. This trend continued into the 1970s and never died, as the emergence of punk rock in the

Energy crisis hits the West. A long queue of cars at one of the few petrol stations open in South London in December 1973.

One of the three women Prime Ministers of the decade – Israel's Mrs Golda Meir.

Introduction

second half of the decade illustrates clearly. Yet, in contrast with the sixties, many of the most experimental and original sounds and musicians came to be relegated to the fringes and scorned or rejected by the public at large. The most popular artists of the decade, who sold most records and made most money – often much more than any of the sixties' stars had made – were a new generation of superstars whose appeal depended as much on their image as the quality of their music and who were often despised by more serious musicians for their 'sell out' to commercialism.

In the same way there were plenty of thoughtful plays and films dealing with contemporary themes – and with the ending of censorship, plenty to be shocked about as well – but those that caught public attention often owed more to their glossiness or technical virtuosity than to their message or creativity.

In art and architecture, the cult of modernism that had reached its height with the op-art and concrete and glass of the sixties went out of fashion and was increasingly replaced by a nostalgia for the past. It was as if, as the seventies went on, people looked to the arts less for stimulation than for escapism, either into a fantasy world of excitement, violence and glamour or into a bygone golden age.

The threshold of the eighties

By the end of the decade much had been altered. Old quarrels between nations had been settled and new ones emerged. Women and American Blacks had made significant progress in their fight for equality, although both had fallen far short of their goals. Technology and change were no longer admired for their own sake. Fewer historic buildings were bulldozed in the interests of modernization and less countryside carelessly destroyed to make way for motorways and airport runways. Western society had become quieter and less rebellious. A reaction began to some aspects of the permissive society, and in the USA a religious revival was underway. Student rebellion was dead and urban terrorism on the decline, although not in Latin America.

Yet in a way the decade ended on an unexpected note, for the worst predictions about the future did not seem to be coming true. The West had not collapsed. The oil continued to flow, although at a much higher price than before, and western economies were recovering. Only unemployment remained an intractable problem. Doom-watching went out of fashion. Politicians like Margaret Thatcher in Britain and Ronald Reagan in the United States, who were rising to prominence and who were to dominate the eighties, preached optimism. All that was really needed, they argued, was for the West to recover confidence in itself and prosperity would return. Whatever happened in the end, it was clear that 1980 would be a very different year from 1970.

Johnny Rotten of the Sex Pistols. Punk rock and other styles of music became a focus in the late 1970s for the frustrations of young people in a period of recession and rising political tensions.

Black

Palestinians Tired of Waiting

IN SEPTEMBER 1970 the frustration of the Palestinians boiled over. Tired of waiting for the Arab states to crush Israel and win back their land for them, they were ready to take desperate measures to bring their case to world attention.

Ordeal in the Skies

HIJACKERS STRIKE FOUR TIMES
Four hijacks over Western Europe – three succeeded and the other failed after a hijacker was shot dead in a battle over the North Sea – made yesterday the worst day for piracy in the history of civil aviation. Palestinian guerillas have claimed credit.
Headline in *The Times*, 7 September

The unsuccessful attempt took place on an El Al (Israeli Airlines) Boeing 707 bound from Amsterdam to New York. The crew managed to overcome the hijackers, although one guerilla and a steward were killed during the struggle.

The plane then made an emergency landing at London's Heathrow and the surviving guerilla, Leila Khaled, was taken into custody at Ealing police station.

Hostages taken

THE THREE OTHER HIJACKED PLANES were forced to fly to the Middle East. One, which landed in Cairo, was blown up on the runway minutes after the passengers had been allowed to leave via the escape shutes. The two others – one German and one Swiss – were taken to an airfield 40 miles north of Amman, the capital of Jordan. Two days later they were joined by a British plane hijacked that day. Soon afterwards, the women, children and sick (except the Israeli ones) were released, leaving 310 passengers and crew as hostages. Units of the Jordanian army quickly surrounded the aircraft but were helpless to intervene once they found out that sticks of gelignite had been planted on each plane.

The hijackers make their demands

THE GUERILLAS belonged to the Popular Front for the Liberation of Palestine, which had broken away from the more moderate Palestine Liberation Organization (PLO). In return for the lives of the hostages, they demanded the release of three Palestinians serving long prison sentences in Switzerland for an attack on an Israeli airliner in Zurich in 1969, three in gaol in West Germany, and Leila Khaled. If these demands were not met within 72 hours, the aircraft would be blown up with everyone on board. But as soon as it looked as though these conditions might be met, they raised the stakes and demanded the release of *all* Palestinians held in Israel, which the Israeli government refused to do.

In Jerusalem Mrs Meir, the Prime Minister, had earlier made it clear that Israel was unwilling to release the guerillas. 'Now they expect us to march them out of gaol ceremoniously', she said in a speech, 'so that they can recross the border and resume their crimes.'
Reported in *The Times*, 10 September

Although the Red Cross twice managed to get the deadline extended, deadlock had been reached. The attention of the whole world was now riveted on Jordan.

Ordeal in the desert (left). Passengers from the hijacked Swiss airliner in Jordan listen to a speech from one of their captors. Soon after this the women and children were set free.

Airport security tightened (right): a passenger has her luggage closely searched by security guards at Brussels Airport, September 1970.

September

King Hussein intervenes

SUDDENLY ON 12 SEPTEMBER all but 54 of the hostages were released. The remainder – a mixture of British, Swiss, German, American and Israeli males – were taken by their captors to Amman and hidden there. Their plight seemed more precarious than ever. The three planes – £10,000,000 of hardware – were blown up where they stood.

King Hussein of Jordan was alarmed. After the wars of 1948 and 1967, 700,000 refugees from Palestine had settled in camps on the outskirts of Amman, over which the King's government had little control. The hijack had been planned from there. Now there was a distinct danger that Jordan might get the blame and the Israelis take revenge on her. The Palestinians decided Hussein must be brought under control once and for all. On 16 September he appointed Field Marshal Habis Al-Majali as

commander-in-chief with orders to bring the refugee camps under proper control. The PLO leader, Yasser Arafat, ordered them to retaliate and fierce fighting broke out between Palestinians and the Jordanian army. For eight days Amman became a battleground.

Six days of savage and relentless fighting have left a mark on this city that even time may not erase. It now seems that casualties will not be less than 15,000, a high proportion of them deaths.

There is no sign that the guerillas will surrender. Those who argued that King Hussein could eliminate the Palestinians from his kingdom without great suffering have been proved wrong. What is going on now in Jordan is a civil war in which those who are suffering most are the innocent.
Report by *Times* correspondent Paul Martin, who was trapped in the Intercontinental Hotel in Amman for 8 days, *The Times*, 24 September

Hostages released

GRADUALLY THE JORDANIAN ARMY came out on top and took control of the city street by street. One by one, all except six of the hostages were discovered during house to house searches, and released. Arab politicians, anxious to heal the breach in Arab unity, sent General Numeiry of the Sudan to mediate. On 27 September, in the presence of most of the Arab leaders assembled in Cairo, Hussein and Arafat signed a truce, under which both the guerillas and the Jordanian army moved out of Amman, leaving the city once again under a civil police force. A commission under the Tunisian Prime Minister was set up to organize relief for the suffering civilians and work out a long-term solution. The immediate crisis was over and a fragile peace returned to war-torn Jordan.

The lessons of September

ALTHOUGH THE PALESTINIANS suffered a bitter defeat in the full glare of world attention, they could also claim 'Black September' (as they came to call it) as a kind of success, for on 30 September the European governments released the seven imprisoned Arabs. The lesson that terrorist tactics paid off was not lost on other embattled minorities around the world.

The nature of air-travel changed for good. The searching of passengers and luggage by magnetic screens and other electronic equipment became routine at major airports. At some, armed soldiers with automatic weapons and live ammunition stood guard.

Shopping basket election

IN THE ELECTION CALLED FOR JUNE, Tory Party leader Edward Heath made the poor performance of the economy under the 1964-70 Labour government his main theme. Too much attention, he argued, had been paid to spending and redistributing wealth and not enough on creating it in the first place. In the long run this was bound to be disastrous.

You cannot provide compassion on the cheap and you cannot make a nation richer by making it poorer. We shall end that mistake.
It is not a question of the head ruling the heart but rather of the head making possible the better life for all on which the rest of us have set our hearts.
Edward Heath in an interview with journalists, 17 June, reported in *The Times*, 18 June

The Conservatives would give the economy a kick-start by refusing to prop up unprofitable firms, refusing pay rises that were not 'earned' by increased productivity and reorganizing the social services so that the money went to those who really needed it. The

Press dubbed it the 'shopping basket election'. The Conservatives won with a majority of 68.

The moment of victory! Edward Heath on the morning after his party's election success.

The end of an era?

ON 27 OCTOBER the new Conservative policy took off in Chancellor Anthony Barber's 'mini-budget', which contained wide-ranging cuts in public expenditure. What caused the most uproar were not the big cuts but relatively minor ones such as the abolition of free school milk for the over-sevens and the introduction of entrance charges for museums and art galleries. Many people felt that an era in British life was coming to a close. Depending on their point of view, they accused the Heath government of being hard-faced young men intent on destroying Britain's humane social welfare system, or praised them as

realists who would teach the feather-bedded British that they couldn't have what they didn't work for.

Surely the introduction of admission charges to our national galleries and museums is a change for the worse. There must be many who, like myself, drop into the National Gallery for some ten minutes to see some newly-displayed picture. Is such use of our galleries to be discouraged? . . .
And I have always been proud to tell my foreign friends that we share these privileges with guests from overseas. We do not regard tourists merely with mercenary eyes! I have felt that in this matter of free admission we were more civilised than other nations.
Letter to *The Daily Telegraph*, 31 October

A second try at Europe

SEVEN YEARS AFTER A FRENCH VETO had sabotaged her first attempt, Britain reapplied for membership of the European Economic Community (Common Market).

The war spreads into Cambodia

PRESIDENT NIXON, who had promised to take America out of the Vietnam War, was responsible for its spread in May 1970, when American troops invaded neutral Cambodia. On television, Nixon justified his decision by the need to wipe out Vietcong bases inside Cambodia before American troops could be safely withdrawn. It seemed as if another small country was about to be devastated by the war to which no one could find a solution.

Is the United States falling apart?

THE CAMBODIAN INVASION sparked off anti-war protests on American campuses on an even larger scale than in 1968. At Kent State University in Ohio National Guardsmen, sent in to control a demonstration, opened fire wildly and killed four students – who, it was later revealed, were not even involved in the rioting. The alienation of young Americans, the spread of the Black Power movement and racial tensions in the cities led many Americans to doubt whether the United States could survive long in its present form. 'This society', said Mayor Lindsay of New York in April, 'is practically on the point of spiritual and possibly even of physical breakdown'.

Old enemies reconciled

ONE OF THE MANY quarrels outstanding from the Second World War was settled on 7 December when Chancellor Brandt of West Germany signed a treaty with Poland 'for the normalizing of our mutual relations'. After more than 20 years Germany accepted the boundary changes that had taken place in 1945. Before signing the treaty, Brandt laid a wreath at the memorial to the victims of the Warsaw Ghetto and went down on his knees in an unrehearsed gesture of repentance for German war crimes. He called this policy of reconciliation with Germany's eastern neighbours 'Ostpolitik'.

Repentance and reconciliation. Chancellor Brandt of West Germany kneeling at the Polish National Memorial in Warsaw.

Momentous election in Chile

THE CHILEAN ELECTIONS in September were won by a left-wing coalition led by the Marxist, Dr Salvador Allende, who became the world's first democratically elected Communist President. This result was regarded with horror by much of the wealthy Chilean middle class. There were attempts to incite the army into staging a coup to stop Allende taking office, and the Commander-in-Chief, General Schneider – who refused to support such a coup – was assassinated. Allende promised he would combine socialism with respect for democracy and freedom of speech.

Women protest! Feminists trying to break up the Miss World contest at the Albert Hall.

Obituaries

TWO IMPORTANT POLITICIANS and one nation died in 1970. In June the 950-day-old Nigerian civil war ended with the surrender of the breakaway state of Biafra. The war had brought a devastating famine to Biafra and thousands of children were still dying of starvation. President Nasser of Egypt, who had led and symbolized the Arab struggle against Israel, died of a heart attack the day after the ending of the Jordanian civil war. He was succeeded by Anwar Sadat. Dr Salazar, dictator of Portugal since 1932, died in July. Under his rule the Portuguese economy had stagnated, civil rights had decayed, and precious resources wasted attempting to cling on to African colonies at a time when other colonial powers were granting independence. He was succeeded as dictator by Dr Caetano.

Terrorism in Canada

UNUSUALLY, CANADIAN POLITICS hit the world headlines in October when French Canadian separatists campaigning for an independent state of Quebec, kidnapped the British trade commissioner in Montreal, James Cross, and a Canadian minister, Pierre Laporte. Canadian Prime Minister Pierre Trudeau refused to negotiate. Laporte was later murdered, but Cross was rescued by the police after two months in captivity.

Women on the March

THE ANNUAL MISS WORLD contest held in the Albert Hall on 20 November was disrupted by women throwing stink bombs and rotten fruit. They argued that such contests were degrading to women. This was a sign of the emergence of feminism or 'Women's Liberation' as a key political movement of the 1970s.

Love and Music on Isle of Wight

THOSE WHO BELIEVED that the age of the great pop festivals was over were proved wrong in August, when hundreds of thousands gathered on the Isle of Wight for a week-long 'festival of music and love'. Among the performers were Joan Baez, The Who and Jimi Hendrix, making his last public performance before his death in September from a drug overdose. The festival came in for a lot of criticism, as most of the audience avoided paying the entrance fee by camping outside the fenced arena, where the powerfully-amplified music could be heard quite clearly, upsetting many local people.

Society under fire

THE REBELLIOUSNESS AND TURMOIL of the 1960s were far from over by 1970, so it is hardly surprising that some of the most talked-about books and films of the year were highly critical of society. The American film *MASH*, an anti-war black comedy set in Korea but with unmistakable parallels to Vietnam, condemned not only war but also the corrupt society that gave rise to it. It made the reputations of two young actors, Elliot Gould and Donald Sutherland.

Charles Reich, a professor of law at Yale University, published *The Greening of America*, in which he predicted that the youth culture was producing a new kind of American – more concerned with human relationships and the beauty of the world around them than with status and material success. As more and more of these 'Consciousness III' people emerged, he argued, American society would be permanently transformed – for the better. The book made a great impact at the time, although in the long run Reich's predictions did not come true.

S.S. Great Britain comes Home

JACK HAYWARD, a British businessman, put up £150,000 to bring the *S.S. Great Britain*, the world's first propeller-driven iron steamship, back from the Falkland Islands, where she had been abandoned as a wreck in 1886. On 5 July she arrived back in Bristol, from where she had been launched in 1843, after an 8000-mile tow across the Atlantic. It was intended to restore her as she had been in her heyday.

Dissident Wins Nobel Prize

THE NOBEL PRIZE FOR LITERATURE was won by the Russian author, Alexander Solzhenitsyn, for his two novels, *Cancer Ward* and *The First Circle*, which show the struggle of ordinary men and women to retain their humanity under a repressive political system. Neither book was published in the Soviet Union.

South Africa and Sport

SOUTH AFRICA'S apartheid policy was making it more and more difficult for her to take part in international sporting events. When a visa was refused to black American tennis-player, Arthur Ashe, to play in the South African championships, South Africa was banned from the Davis Cup. In Britain a 'Stop the Seventy Tour' campaign successfully prevented the visit of the South African cricket team. In fact, by the end of the decade South Africa was almost totally excluded from international competition.

Shocks!

THE VIRTUAL ABOLITION of censorship by the end of the sixties was felt in full force in 1970. Two productions that caused ripples of shock were the stage musical *Oh! Calcutta* and the film *Women in Love*, which gave British cinema audiences their first views of full frontal male nudity. Most people were fairly unconcerned but others were not so sure that complete artistic freedom was a good thing.

The idea that man has outgrown the need for restraints is the most piteous and dangerous fiction that has ever deluded the human mind. For it is necessary to guard men from being exposed to stress, psychologically and morally, just as we try to create conditions that rule out his exposure to atmospheric and other pollutants.
Letter to *The Times*, from the Bishop of Peterborough, 29 July

Sporting News

THE WORLD CUP held in Mexico was won by Brazil for the third time, who were then allowed to keep the trophy. Pessimists had predicted dull matches dominated by the well-drilled defences of the European sides, but the final, in which Brazil beat Italy 4–1, was a triumph of daring, attacking football. The legendary Pele was one of the stars. In the quarter-finals England lost to West Germany after leading 2–0.

Muhammad Ali, who had been stripped of his world heavy-weight title in 1967 after his refusal to do military service, won his two come-back fights, clearing the way for a bout with the current world champion, Joe Frazier.

In September, the Austrian racing driver Jochen Rindt was killed during practice for the Italian Grand Prix. As no driver had passed his tally of points by the end of the season, Rindt became motor racing's first posthumous World Champion.

Drama in Space

AFTER TWO SUCCESSFUL MOONSHOTS public interest was beginning to wane. All this changed in a few days in April, when it was brought home to the world afresh just how dangerous man's ventures into space really were. Three days out and 300,000 km from earth, an explosion in *Apollo 13*, bound for the moon, crippled the main ship and forced the astronauts James Lovell, Fred Haise and Jack Sweigert to evacuate into the lunar module, which had to act as a sort of space lifeboat. Three hours later the module's own oxygen and water supply failed, leaving the crew totally dependent on emergency supplies.

Tuesday 14 April, 05.41 BST
Mission Control (Houston) – We figure you've got about 15 minutes worth of power in the command module. So we want you to start getting over to the Lunar Module and getting some power on there. Are you ready to begin your procedure?
Apollo 13 – Okay.
Mission Control – Apollo, this is Houston. We'd like you to start making your way over to the Lunar Module now.
Apollo 13 – Fred and Jim are over in the Lunar Module.
Mission Control – Okay, Jack, thank you.
Apollo 13 – This is Jack. We've got the Lunar Module power on. Okay. You still with us Houston? Houston, are you ready?
Mission Control – Reading you loud and clear, Jack.
Part of conversation between Jack Sweigert, pilot of the Command Module, and Mission Control at the height of the emergency.
Reported in *The Times*, 15 April

For 85 hours, while the astronauts made the journey to earth, the world held its breath. On 14 April, after a perfect splashdown in the Pacific, they were picked up safe and well. The cause of the trouble was later discovered to be two minute thermostat switches that had been wrongly wired. *Apollo 14*, scheduled for October, was postponed until 1971.

New hope for kidney patients

BY 1970 the revolutionary heart transplant operation pioneered by Dr Christian Bernard had proved a disappointment. On the other hand, improved anti-rejection drugs and tissue-typing techniques had made kidney transplants almost routine. Of 19 patients who received new kidneys at the University of California medical centre in the first half of 1970, 15 were back at work by the middle of the year – a success rate of 80 per cent compared with only 38 per cent between 1965 and 1969.

Oil Strike in North Sea

AFTER YEARS OF SUCCESSFUL DRILLING, a big oil strike was made in the Norwegian part of the North Sea. The Ekofisk Field, predicted to produce 300,000 tons a day, was the largest oil field in Europe and (it was claimed) might turn out to be one of the largest in the world.

After three tense days, the Apollo 13 astronauts climb out of their spacecraft after a safe landing in the Pacific.

Dawn of the microchip age

IN 1970 the first microprocessor was patented by the Intel Corporation of the United States. This had been made possible by the invention of the silicon chip in 1961, which enabled the main calculating functions of a computer to be contained on a single ¼in-square chip. Other equally small chips could provide the machine's memory banks. When input and output devices like keyboards and display screens were added, the result was an entire computer system small enough to sit on a desk-top and potentially cheap enough for even the smallest business to afford. A revolution in the processing and retrieval of information was about to begin. Cheap pocket calculators – made possible by the silicon chip – first went on sale in the US in this year.

Environment at Risk

IN JULY both New York and Tokyo were hit by life-threatening smogs when pollution caused by industrial and vehicle waste gases created an oily, yellow fog that shut out sunlight and shut in heat. In Tokyo, thousands of people visited hospital everyday with bronchitis and eye irritation, while in New York so many people turned up their air-conditioning that power cuts were threatened. After decades of thoughtless affluence and technological progress, people began to ask themselves whether 'progress' was always an unmixed blessing. For the first time the fate of the environment became a subject of serious political debate. The BBC's *Doomwatch* regularly drew an audience of 12 million.

1971 China comes in

Twenty years of Emnity

EVER SINCE the Communist takeover in 1949 China had been hostile to the West, especially the United States. This emnity had reached new heights during the Cultural Revolution of 1966-70. In return, the United States had recognized the Nationalist government on Taiwan as the 'true' China and given her military and diplomatic support.

Ping-pong Diplomacy

IN APRIL 1971 the American table-tennis team competing in the world championships in Japan were astonished to receive an invitation from the People's Republic team to visit China. They would be the first Americans to go there since 1949. The reason for this dramatic about-face was probably China's bitter quarrel with the Soviet Union, which had begun in 1960. To be on bad terms with both the Superpowers was just too risky.

From the start the sportsmen were overwhelmed by the cordiality of their hosts. They were received at the airport by no less a person that Prime Minister Zhou Enlai and awarded the honorary status of diplomatic envoys. This visit, he told them, marked a new departure in relations between the peoples of China and the United States.

New Horizons

ALL OVER THE WEST Governments welcomed the new Chinese attitude. President Nixon, once a noted anti-Communist, lifted the ban on visas for Americans wishing to visit China. Crowds of journalists, eager to see what life was really like inside the Communist giant, streamed in. They found the contrasts with the West endlessly fascinating. China herself reconnected the direct telephone links with London that had been broken in 1949, and apologized for the burning down of the British Embassy in Beijing during the Cultural Revolution.

It's such a relief to visit a country where they don't have many *things*. The Chinese have few automobiles, for example. A 'service station' here is a place where neighbours provide and deliver food or other necessities to the sick or working couples who have no time to shop before dinner.

The bicycle is the principle means of transportation in the cities and the dominant sound is the tinkling of thousands of bicycle bells. The Chinese are always telling you how much better things are than they used to be and they are almost childlike in their wonder and thankfulness for small mercies. . . Compared to the West, these days, all this seems rather tame and old-fashioned, but it has great beauty and charm.

Report by the American journalist, James Preston, published in *The Times*, 19 August

Kissinger goes to visit Beijing

IN JULY it was reported that Henry Kissinger, Nixon's National Security Adviser who was on a round-the-world trip, was resting at a remote resort in Pakistan and trying to shake off a stomach upset. In fact, as the world soon discovered, he was on a secret 20-hour trip to Beijing. Six days later, Nixon told the astonished American people on television that he had accepted 'with pleasure' an invitation to visit China before May 1972. The date was later confirmed as 21 February.

As I have pointed out on a number of occasions over the past three years, there can be no stable and enduring peace without the participation of the People's Republic of China and its 750 million people . . . any nation can be our friend without being any other nation's enemy. It is my profound conviction that all nations will gain from a reduction of tensions and a better relationship between the United States and the People's Republic of China.

It is in this spirit that I will undertake what I deeply hope will be a journey for peace – peace not just for our generation but for future generations on the earth we share together.

Part of Nixon's nationwide broadcast on US television, 16 July

from the cold

Alarm in Moscow

IN SPITE OF THE REASSURANCES, this announcement was greeted with trepidation in Moscow and Taiwan.

China was accused tonight in the foreign affairs magazine *New Times* of . . . betraying Communist world interests to curry favour with the United States. Beijing was trying to establish itself as the dominant world power in the old tradition by which China was viewed as the centre of the world.
From the Moscow correspondent of *The Times*, 22 April

China enters the United Nations

ON 19 OCTOBER the annual Albanian motion for the admission of China to the United Nations and the expulsion of Taiwan was once again presented to the General Assembly. For the first time ever, the United States did not veto it outright. The debate was fierce and lasted six days, however, for the American delegate, George Bush, argued strongly that Taiwan be allowed to stay in her own right as the representative of an alternative Chinese state. This compromise was rejected and the Nationalists eventually settled the argument by walking out in disgust. The People's Republic was then duly voted into the United Nations by 76 votes to 35 with 17 abstentions.

Forbidden City – forbidden no longer. With the improved relations between Beijing and the West, China became more accessible to foreign visitors.

A safer world?

These events were no magic answer to world tensions. Sino-American relations were still hampered by US support for Taiwan. China and the USSR remained bitter enemies. Alongside his desire for world peace, Nixon saw a golden opportunity to play the two Communist giants off against each other to American advantage. The political situation in China itself remained volatile. In the autumn the Defence Minister, Lin Biao, disappeared in mysterious circumstances. It was rumoured that he had tried and failed to oust Zhou Enlai, generally presumed to be the architect of the new policy. For the moment Zhou had come out on top, but no one knew how long that would last. In spite of everything, however, most people felt that this sudden and surprising change in Chinese policy had made the world just that little bit safer.

'Kill the Bill'

IN 1971 the stage seemed set for confrontation between the government and the unions. In February the postmen went back to work in defeat after a 47-day strike, the longest national stoppage since the war. The government treated this as a victory for its new 'get tough' policy, but there were those who pointed out that other unions with more industrial 'muscle' might be tougher to crack.

The lynchpin of the government's strategy was its Industrial Relations Bill, which put limits on the right to strike and aimed to outlaw wildcat stoppages. An Industrial Relations court, with all the powers of a court of law, was set up to enforce the new system. Trade unionists regarded it as an infringement of their democratic rights, and on 1 March 100,000 gathered in Trafalgar Square to hear TUC Secretary, Vic Feather, announce a 'Kill the Bill' campaign.

Britain goes decimal

CHAOS WAS PREDICTED for 15 February 1971, when Britain abandoned her traditional pound, shillings and pence for decimal currency. The forecasts of doom ranged from the reasonable (like the fear that shopkeepers would take advantage of the changeover to put up prices) to the bizarre. In fact, 'D-Day' passed off remarkably smoothly and good-humouredly.

Chief Superintendent William Paterson of Bournemouth police fears that shoppers crossing roads will be too busy counting their change to watch for cars. He has asked the British Accident Prevention Committee to issue a warning of 'decimal deaths'. From the *Daily Mail*, 4 February

Britain's new money: Lord Fiske, chairman of the Decimal Currency Board, with the new 5p coin that was introduced in 1968 in readiness for D-Day in 1971.

The Commons Vote 'Yes'

ON 25 OCTOBER the Commons approved the terms of British membership of the EEC. The date for formal admission was set for 1 January 1973.

Internment in Ulster

THE BRITISH PUBLIC was increasingly bewildered by the developing tragedy in Northern Ireland, to which there seemed to be no solution. Justice for Catholics could not be achieved in the face of Protestant opposition, while a total British withdrawal would leave the way open for Protestants to be forced against their will into a united Ireland. The British troops were blamed for this impasse, local Catholics turned against them and support for the IRA grew. A guerilla campaign of attacks on soldiers and bomb outrages in Protestant areas began. In August the army tried to break the IRA once and for all by rounding up all suspected members and imprisoning them indefinitely without trial. But the killing went on. Over the next few weeks the IRA tied up over 12,500 soldiers in street battles, killing several civilian by-standers in the process.

A girl aged 17 months was shot dead tonight as a wave of random terrorism shooting swept through Belfast. The child, Angela Gallagher, from a Roman Catholic family, and her sister aged 7 were pushing a small push-chair along Iveagh Drive . . . in the Falls Road area. Four soldiers on foot-patrol were passing by.

Shots were fired at the soldiers from a car. One bullet . . . passed through the bottom of the skirt of the older girl and hit Angela Gallagher in the head. She was taken to the Children's hospital and found to be dead on arrival.
Report in *The Times*, 4 September

A familiar sight in Northern Ireland; the army helping to evacuate a row of burnt-out houses.

Civil war in Pakistan

IN 1947 Pakistan had been created out of the Muslim areas of British India. As a result the country was made up of two parts, East and West, thousands of miles apart and very different in history and culture. More people lived in East Pakistan or Bengal than in the West, but it was Westerners who were in control. Lead by the Awami League Party under Sheikh Mujibur Rahman, demands for independence grew in the East.

In December 1971 Pakistan had tried to end 12 years of military dictatorship by holding free elections. These were won overwhelmingly by the East Pakistan Awami League Party, led by Sheikh Mujibur Rahman. The League wanted autonomy for the East, and, predictably, President Yahya Khan refused to accept the result and the right of Sheikh Mujibur to become Prime Minister of all Pakistan. In March he outlawed the Awami League, declared their leader a traitor, and sent in the army.

The Bengalis were no match for professional troops. In four weeks of fighting they were defeated and thousands killed. The victorious soldiers from West Pakistan behaved as though they were on enemy territory and committed atrocities. Over four million Bengalis fled to India. Sheikh Mujibur himself was captured and imprisoned in the West to await trial for treason. Guerilla fighters, the Mukhti Bahinis, carried on the struggle behind the lines in occupied East Pakistan.

India Intervenes

THE FLOOD OF REFUGEES stretched India's resources to the limit. In June a cholera epidemic broke out in the camps that nearly spread to nearby Calcutta. Eager to solve this problem and at the same time harm her old enemy Pakistan, India sent aid to the Mukhti Bahinis. On 3 December full-scale war broke out and Indian troops swept into East Bengal. Dacca, the capital, fell on the 16th, the West Pakistani army surrendered and India handed the country over to its inhabitants. With emotions running high, the bloodshed was not quite over, the Mukhti Bahinis now took revenge on the Bihari minority, some of whom had collaborated during the occupation.

India's Prime Minister, Mrs Gandhi, talks to troops fighting in East Pakistan in a war that was to change the political map of the region and create a new nation.

Secret documents published in US

THE REVERBERATIONS OF THE VIETNAM war continued to haunt American politics. The biggest shock of 1971 was in June, when the *New York Times* published extracts from a secret study commissioned by the Pentagon (The Defence Department) into the history of American involvement in South-East Asia. It was revealed that Presidents from Eisenhower to Nixon had constantly lied to Americans about the causes and course of the war. Americans' respect for their government reached a new low, and Daniel Ellsberg, who had leaked the documents to the newspapers, became a kind of national hero. Relations between President and the press, already bad, deteriorated further – something that was to have the greatest effect on Nixon's future.

The world's greatest democracy, the creation of Jefferson and Lincoln, was dragged into the South-East Asian mud by quarrelsome generals, black marketeers and drug pushers, who were thousands of miles away.
From the *Pentagon Papers*

Swiss women enter politics

THE PROGRESS OF WOMEN towards social and political equality took a step forward when, in November, Swiss women were allowed to vote for the first time in the federal elections. Earlier in the year, Swiss men had voted 2–1 in favour of the change in a referendum. The first women deputies – 11 out of a total of 200 – took their seats in the Parliament in Berne.

In a shock result in Norway, a feminist party, campaigning for better nursery provision and safer roads, won control of Oslo city council.

Cinema

1971 WAS A BAD YEAR financially for the cinema. Facing competition from television, admissions to the British cinema fell to 193 million, compared with a peak of 1,514 million in 1943. This pattern was repeated in the United States. While the year produced its crop of socially critical or sexually explicit films (some good and some not so good), the surprise hit of 1971 was the sentimental *Love Story*, starring Ryan O'Neal and Ali MacGraw.

New films of the year

Tora, Tora, Tora, an old-style glossy war movie.

The Music Lovers, directed by Ken Russell: an idiosyncratic version of the life of the composer, Tchaikovsky, full of unnecessary sex and violence.

Little Big Man, starring Dustin Hoffman; *Soldier Blue*, two re-examinations of the relationship between American Indians & White Men. For once the Indians emerge with dignity.

Walkabout, an Australian film about the survival of two children stranded in the desert. A dignified view of Aborigine culture.

A Clockwork Orange, directed by Stanley Kubrick, based on a novel by Anthony Burgess.

The Last Picture Show, a tale of small-town American life in the 1950s. The first of the nostalgic movies.

Klute, psychological thriller starring Jane Fonda and Donald Sutherland.

Musicals

TWO VERY DIFFERENT MUSICALS hit the headlines. *Jesus Christ, Superstar* which opened in London that year, was the first big hit for the song-writing team of Tim Rice and Andrew Lloyd-Webber. The theme of the musical is that Christ's career was ultimately a failure. While much criticized in Church circles, it proved immensely popular, and the album of its songs sold over 3 million copies. After 2,844 performances, *Fiddler on the Roof* – a sentimental picture of life and love in a Russian Jewish ghetto – became Broadway's longest-running musical ever.

Hot pants and fatigues

WHEN THE FASHION HOUSES tried to bring back feminine styles by reintroducing below-the-knee hemlines, classic suits for daytime wear and flowing evening dresses, there was a mass revolt among the young against the disappearance of the mini-skirt. 'Hot pants', ultra-short culottes that were worn even in the coldest weather, became the rage. The anti-establishment young on the campuses continued to wear 'protest clothes' such as army surplus fatigues, dungarees and deliberately beat-up jeans.

Hot pants – worn in all weathers.

Feminist classic published

THE FLOOD OF FEMINIST LITERATURE produced one of its classics with *The Female Eunuch* by Germaine Greer. Women, she argued, had been conditioned for centuries to suppress their abilities and regard themselves as weak and dependent, and this conditioning had its roots in the family. Attempts to liberate women by giving them the vote or through male-led revolutions like the Russian and Chinese ones had failed because they had not touched the real problem. Only by developing her own unique strengths and freeing herself from men and male values could women be truly free. Many people were outraged at this threat to traditional lifestyles.

The housewife who must wait for the success of world revolution for her liberty might be excused for losing hope, while conservative political methods can invent no way in which the economically necessary unit of the one-man family could be diversified. But there is another dimension in which she can find motive and cause for action, although she may not find a blue-print for Utopia. She could begin not by changing the world, but by reassessing herself.

The Female Eunuch, 1971

Stars Old and New

MUHAMMAD ALI failed in his first attempt to win back his heavyweight title when he was beaten on points by Joe Frazier. The Ladies Singles at Wimbledon were won by 20-year-old Evonne Goolagong from Australia, whose flowing, instinctive tennis crushed the three-times champion Margaret Court. British yachtsman Chay Blyth sailed around the world from west to east single-handed against the prevailing winds and currents. A crowd of thousands greeted his arrival back in Southampton after 292 days at sea.

Tragedy in space

IN APRIL THE USSR put the world's first space station – Salyut I – into orbit. Cosmonauts would now be able to stay in space much longer than was possible on ordinary spacecraft and to carry out experiments on the effect of prolonged weightlessness on the human body. This knowledge would be essential if interplanetary flight were ever to become a reality.

On 6 June a spaceship – *Soyuz II* – docked with Salyut. Three cosmonauts spent 23 days on board carrying out tests in zero gravity. Then tragedy struck. After an apparently normal re-entry the cosmonauts were found dead in their seats. The cause seems to have been a sudden drop in air pressure inside the cabin, causing fatal embolism air bubbles in the cosmonauts' blood vessels.

Supersonic age begins

THE ANGLO-FRENCH supersonic aircraft Concorde made a successful test flight on 19 May, covering the 400 miles from Toulouse to Paris in 19 minutes, at twice the speed of sound. President Pompidou of France was on board. The flight was a technological triumph for a plane whose early production had been dogged by difficulties, but serious doubts remained about its future. It was so expensive to run that it might never make a profit and fears were being expressed about the noise it made on take-off and breaking the sound barrier (sonic boom). A number of major airports including JFK in New York had hinted that they might not allow it to land. Sixteen planes were on the production line but few had yet been sold. Labour and Liberal MPs in Britain pressed for the project to be cancelled. The American equivalent, the Boeing SST, had already been scrapped.

Alternative Medicine

AMERICAN DOCTORS VISITING CHINA brought back startling stories about the way the Chinese used the age-old art of acupuncture in modern surgery. Acupuncture works on the principle that pain can be relieved by using long needles to apply pressure to certain nerve points in the body, which are often a long way from where the pain is actually felt. Observers reported seeing open heart surgery and tumours removed with no other anaesthetic being used. The patient was conscious throughout and told the surgeon when numbness began and when to apply more pressure. No one really understood how it worked or whether this technique could be transferred to the West as an alternative to expensive and potentially dangerous drugs. It might be that acupuncture's effect was psychological and only worked if the patient had complete faith in it.

Concorde returning from night trials near Toulouse.

The cholesterol debate

The visitor is greeted by a colour slide showing the fatty chaos in a heart prone to attack. The most telling argument is a pair of pictures, one showing a slide of the heart of a child aged one, with light streaming through three clear windows leading to the main artery. The other shows the same heart 64 years later, a fatty red and yellow mess reminiscent of a Picasso nightmare.

The 'nightmare' is created, the exhibition claims, by a combination of lack of exercise, smoking, hereditary factors and the wrong sort of fatty foods. The average Briton eats an average 21 lbs of butter compared with 14 lbs of margarine every year. Butter, being a concentrated animal fat, is the worst possible food, it is claimed, for creating the high level of cholesterol that can kill.

Report in *The Times*, 18 May, on a 4-day exhibition organized by van der Berghs, the makers of Flora margarine. In what way can it be said that the organizers have a vested interest in the heart disease debate?

Although there was still much argument, especially among food manufacturers with vested interests, scientific evidence was fast coming down on the side of the theory that heart disease was not just due to bad luck closely linked to a person's lifestyle. A revolution in eating and exercise habits was about to take off.

Detente, but the

Detente: Nixon and Mao met in Beijing in February.

A new word – detente

1972 SAW A REMARKABLE SHOW of cordiality between the superpowers, who had concluded that a nuclear world was such a dangerous place that it was in their interests to get along together. They agreed to cooperate in practical ways and not to let ideological differences disrupt world peace. This policy of Detente was a great turnabout for President Nixon, who had been a noted anti-Communist in his youth. Only between the Soviet Union and China did relations not improve.

First stop – Beijing

NIXON'S FIRST GOODWILL VISIT was to Beijing, where he was entertained on a lavish scale and had a private meeting with Party chairman, Mao Zedong. Nothing concrete was agreed at the talks and the thorny problem of Taiwan remained unsettled, but the visit did much to dispel decades of mutual distrust. During a walk on the Great Wall, Nixon was applauded by his hosts when he said that there should be 'no walls between peoples on ideological grounds'. Two giant pandas, Ling-ling and Hsing-hsing, were presented as a gift to the American people.

Summit meeting in Moscow

NIXON PAID AN EIGHT-DAY VISIT to Moscow in May, the first-ever by a serving American President. Agreements were signed for joint projects in science, technology, health and environmental protection. A joint space programme was planned for 1975, and there were promises of more cultural and educational exchanges. Vietnam, which might have been a bone of contention, was deliberately ignored by both sides. It was not considered risking world peace for.

SALT Arms Limitation Treaty signed

THE GREATEST COUP of the Moscow summit was the first Strategic Arms Limitation Treaty (SALT I). Both sides promised to pin their long-range nuclear weapons to agreed limits for the next five years. The Soviet Union was to be allowed a maximum of 62 nuclear weapon-carrying submarines, the USA 44; the Soviet Union 1700 inter-continental ballistic missiles, the USA 1,504. American inferiority in numbers was compensated for by multiple warheads and superior technology. No provision was made for on-site inspection. It was optimistically assumed that any violations would be picked up by spy satellites. The treaty came nowhere near ridding the world of nuclear weapons, but it was seen as a hopeful start. It was the first arms limitation treaty since the Test Ban Treaty of 1963.

Although there were differences of principle between the two powers, there were also 'objective factors giving them similar interests', President Podgorny declared in his speech at the Kremlin banquet.

These required the two powers 'to act in such a way as to ward off the danger of a global war from Soviet – American relations'. They should do everything possible to rid their relationship of 'all that complicated it in the past and burdens it now'. The Soviet Union deems it 'possible and desirable to establish not merely good but friendly relations between the USSR and the US, certainly not at the expense of third countries or peoples.'
President Podgorny's speech at the Kremlin banquet in honour of President Nixon, as reported in *The Times*, 22 May

war goes on

Detente: Nixon and Brezhnev (right) sign a treaty of co-operation between their two countries in May.

A breach in the wall

WITH ACTIVE Russian encouragement, Detente was reflected on a smaller scale in Europe, where Communist East Germany agreed to cooperate with Brandt's Ostpolitik. The two Germanys, who had refused to acknowledge the other's existence for over 20 years, signed a 'Basic Treaty', recognizing each other's right to exist and promising to cooporate in technological and environmental matters. For an eight-day period over Easter, the Berlin Wall was opened for the first time since its erection in 1961. Long-separated familes and friends could be reunited for a few days.

Reunited – if only temporarily; the Berlin Wall opens at Easter to allow West Berliners to visit relatives in the East. Over half a million crossed over before it was closed again eight days later.

The Vietnam War goes on

WITH THE COMING OF DETENTE, the Russians and Chinese more or less abandoned the North Vietnamese to sort our their quarrel with the Americans on their own. Although desperate to pull out, the Americans still failed to work out how this could be done without leaving South Vietnam in the lurch. In the process of disengaging they appeared to become more embroiled than ever. When the Vietcong launched a major offensive in April, Nixon ordered the bombing of civilian as well as military targets in the North. The port of Haiphong, through which most of North Vietnam's supplies came, was mined. When fighting flared up again in October, the US dropped 800,000 tons of bombs on the North, compared to 763,000 in the whole of 1971.

World News

Industrial unrest in Britain; picketing miners and police clash outside a Gas Board depot in Saltley, Birmingham. The miners are trying to bring the depot to a halt by preventing supplies brought by lorry getting in, tactics which eventually give them victory in the 1972 strike.

Industrial troubles

A MINERS' STRIKE OVER A PAY CLAIM had a very different outcome from that of the postmen a year earlier. The miners did not only close down the pits but also used mass picketing to stop supplies of coal and oil reaching the power stations. The government declared the tactic illegal but seemed powerless to stop it. Electricity had to be rationed by means of power cuts on a rota basis of three hours on, three hours off. In the end the government gave in and set up an independent inquiry, which gave the miners the 47% they demanded and which many people thought they deserved. After this, the Heath government brought in a compulsory three-stage policy of wage restraint to apply to everyone and to be spread out over two years.

The Industrial Relations Bill caused trouble in June when the Industrial Relations court sent three London

Bloody Sunday

THE 'TROUBLES' IN ULSTER now took a turn for the worse, when civil rights marchers in Londonderry clashed with troops on 31 January. Soldiers fired over 200 rounds of ammunition and thirteen marchers were killed, all of them men between the ages of 16 and 41. Each side blamed the other for starting the violence. The incident damaged relations between the army and local Catholics beyond repair and strengthened the position of the IRA. On 22 February they retaliated by bombing the officers mess at Aldershot, killing six civilians and one officer. Ulster Protestants retaliated in turn and Northern Ireland was brought to the verge of civil war. The death toll

dockers to jail for contempt, after they had defied a court order to stop picketing the new container depots. Container ports used much less labour than traditional docks and dockers feared that their livelihood was at stake. 35,000 men came out in a sympathy strike, which lasted until the three men were released on 16 August.

for 1972 was 470 compared with 173 in 1971. In an attempt to break the vicious cycle, the Northern Irish Parliament, Stormont, was closed down and Ulster brought under direct rule from London. To William Whitelaw, the Secretary of State for Ulster, fell the unenviable job of keeping the peace between the two sides and reconciling Catholics to British rule.

What happened today is mass murder by the army. Let nobody say they opened fire to retaliate. They shot up a peaceful march. Then they let loose with bloodthirsty gusto at anything that strayed into their sights. This was our Sharpeville and we will never forget it.
Comment by Northern Irish Civil Rights MP, Bernadette Devlin, 1 February

It is not true that we fired indiscriminately into the crowd. We were fired on first. If the army's shooting was as indiscriminate as some people would have you believe, I am sure that a woman or a child would have been hit. All those killed fell into the age bracket from which we have come to expect trouble.
Comment by a spokesman for the army, reported in *The Times*, 1 February

A symbol of the decade; a hooded Palestinian guarding the balcony of the apartment in the Munich Olympic Village where 11 Israeli athletes are held hostage.

Terrorism hits Germany

PROSPEROUS WEST GERMANY suffered an outbreak of urban terrorism that had rather different roots. Under the slogan 'the war is being carried into the residential areas', young revolutionaries calling themselves the Baader-Meinhof gang began a campaign of indiscriminate car bombing that left four dead and 36 injured. The leaders of the gang, Andreas Baader, Ulricke Meinhof and Gudrun Ensslin, were eventually arrested in June.

Shady dealings in American election year

PRESIDENTIAL ELECTIONS were due in November in the US. Nixon was standing again. During the campaign a possible Democratic candidate, George Wallace, was shot by an assassin whose motives were unclear. He was paralysed for life. On 17 June police caught five men red-handed planting bugging devices in Democratic Party headquarters in the Watergate building in Washington. FBI investigators soon discovered that the men were employees of C.R.E.E.P. (The Committee to Re-Elect the President), which was run from the White House. Nixon denied any knowledge of the affair and it had no effect on his popularity. Riding high on his reputation as a peacemaker, he won a landslide victory over the Democrat, George McGovern.

Massacre at the Olympic Games

OF THE MANY ACTS OF TERRORISM to hit the headlines in 1972 the most traumatic took place at the Olympic Games in Munich. Palestinian guerillas calling themselves 'Black September' sneaked into the Olympic village and took eleven Israeli athletes hostage, demanding that the Israeli government release 200 imprisoned Palestinians. In line with her usual policy, Israel refused, and during an attempted rescue by the German police all the hostages were killed. The Games went on as planned, although many people criticized the decision at the time.

No joint act on air piracy

IN OCTOBER Palestinians hijacked a Lufthansa jet at Beirut airport and demanded the release of the surviving Black September men, now in prison in Germany. The German government gave in to these demands, much to the anger of the Israelis. It was now obvious that air piracy would not be stopped unless all nations agreed on a common policy of not giving in to blackmail whatever the cost. But in September a fifteen-nation conference held in Washington failed even to agree on the very modest proposal that signatories suspend air services to any country that harboured hijackers.

A new nation – Bangladesh

SHEIKH MUJIBUR RAHMAN was released in January and returned home in triumph. Before a crowd of tens of thousands at Dacca airport, he proclaimed the new nation of Bangladesh (Land of the Bengalis).

Despite the joy, the future of the new nation was very uncertain. Bangladesh was one of the poorest and most over-populated nations on earth. As the refugees poured back from India, only international aid prevented famine.

The pop music scene

1972 SAW THE RISE of a new generation of super-stars whose appeal depended more on their image and visual appeal than on the originality of their music. Among the new idols were Alice Cooper (who was a man), whose act included rough rock music and simulated killings; Roxy Music; Marc Bolan, whose long curling hair, satin suits and glittery eye-shadow reduced young girls to a hysteria not seen since Beatlemania; Rod Stewart; the British group, Slade; and the teenagers' favourite, 13-year-old Donny Osmond, singer of sickly ballads. David Bowie had been around since the sixties and was considerably more ambitious and inventive musically – though often bracketed with these other 'glam rock' acts. In 1972 he released the famous LP *Ziggy Stardust and the Spiders from Mars*. Some serious musicians dismissed the new stars as commercial gimmicks, who had little to offer that was truly new or creative. A gulf began to open up between mainstream pop, to which most people listened, and the sounds followed by more serious (or older) rock fans.

Outrageous superstar: Alice Cooper in concert in Switzerland.

New magazine launched

A NEW MAGAZINE, *Ms.*, was launched in July. Although advertised as a feminist publication, its editor, Gloria Steinem, saw it not as a 'movement journal' but as a 'medium covering a new phase in human development', of vital interest to anyone who wanted to understand the times. By mid October it had 200,000 subscribers and sold over 300,000 copies per month on the newstands, a phenomenal record for a new magazine. It is still going strong in the USA today.

Munich Olympics

THE SPORTING SIDE of the 1972 Olympic Games was dominated by the Russians, Americans and East Germans, who between them won 103 out of a total of 191 gold medals. Among the stars were American swimmer, Mark Spitz, who broke 7 world records; 15-year-old Shane Gould from Australia who won five gold medals and broke the women's 400m freestyle swimming record; and the little Russian gymnast, Olga Korbutt, whose failure to win first place on the asymmetrical bars caused spectators to boo and whistle for over ten minutes. Britain's only gold medal in athletics was won by Mary Peters from Belfast in the Pentathlon (100m hurdles, shot, high jump, long jump and 200m race).

The lure of the past

ONE OF THE OUTSTANDING artistic events of the year was not concerned with creating anything new but with relics from the distant past. Over a million and a half people visited the British Museum in the spring and summer to view the mummy, sarcophagus and other relics from the tomb of the Egyptian pharaoh, Tutankhamun, who had died around 1340 BC. The exhibition's organizer, the newspaper magnate Lord Thomson, handed the profits over to UNESCO.

American superstars

TWO VERY DIFFERENT faces of American sport were seen in 1972. Bobby Fischer broke the Russian domination of chess when he took the world title from Boris Spassky. His arrogant and unsporting behaviour, however, won him few friends. The baseball world lost a great player who was also a compassionate human being when Roberto Clemente was killed in a plane crash while ferrying supplies to victims of an earthquake in Nicaragua. In his 17 years with the Pittsburgh Pirates he had won the National League batting championship four times and helped the Pirates to win the World Series in 1971. His death left unfulfilled his dreams of building a sports city for unemployed youngsters in his native Puerto Rico.

Some films of 1972

One Day in the Life of Ivan Denisovitch – an adaptation of Solzhenitsyn's short story about life in a Soviet labour camp, starring Tom Courtenay.

The Godfather – starring Marlon Brando and Al Pacino – the saga of an Italian-American Mafia family. The box office hit of the year.

Cabaret – a musical set in the Berlin of the early 1930s, which made stars out of Liza Minnelli and Joel Gray.

The Candidate – starring Robert Redford. A satire on American political life.

The Discreet Charm of the Bourgeoisie – a satire on middle-class life and attitudes, by the veteran Spanish film director Luis Bunuel.

New developments in air travel

HEADLINE-GRABBING hijacks and increased security hid the fact that other important developments were taking place in civil aviation. In 1972 passenger numbers reached record levels. One reason for this was the Boeing 747 'Jumbo' jet, which flew on the Transatlantic route in 1970. It could carry 300-400 people. Another was the growing number of different airlines. Increased competition led to lower prices and put air travel into the reach of more people. Most significant of all, perhaps, the rules laying down who could run charter flights were relaxed and the number of passengers on such flights tripled in number in 1972. Low-budget package holidays and one-off trips to big occasions like the Olympic Games or international football matches became common.

A bad year for air disasters

WITH INCREASED AIR TRAFFIC, there was a dramatic increase in the number of serious accidents. On 14 August the world's worst-ever civil air disaster occurred at Schoenefeld Airport in East Berlin, when a Russian-built plane crashed on take-off killing 156. In October, 176 died in a crash near Moscow and 155 when a Spanish charter plane exploded and disintegrated on the runway at Tenerife. All 118 people on board a British Trident died when it stalled shortly after take-off from Heathrow on 18 June. In the Commons the next day MPs asked some telling questions about air safety in the new era of mass transportation.

Mr McNair Wilson (Walthamstow E., Con.) This is the most appalling tragedy we have had in civil aviation. It could have been just that much worse if the aircraft had fallen on Staines. Is the Minister satisfied with a take-off pattern that allows aircraft that are climbing and therefore most vulnerable to fly so close to a densely-populated area?

Mr Russell Johnston (Inverness, Lib.) While BEA (British European Airways) have a first-class safety record, it seems to be horribly true that when the modern airliner crashes the chances of survival are small. What resources are being directed by BEA or the Minister towards increasing the chances of survival under crash conditions?

Mr Mason (Barnsley, Lab.) The Trident has an excellent safety record but modern aircraft have to make an increasing number of flights. Will the Minister take all possible steps to speed up the enquiries to establish that no structural or engine weaknesses are developing on this type of aircraft?
From the account of the Commons debate on the 19 June, reported in *The Times*, 20 June

A new missile

DESPITE SALT, the superpowers went on developing new and more lethal weapons. In 1972 the Pentagon announced that its submarine-based Poseidon missiles were to be replaced by Tridents, which had a range of 5000 miles, twice that of Poseidon.

Man's earliest ancestor?

IN NORTHERN KENYA the anthropologist, Richard Leakey, found a broken skull and fragments of other bones estimated to be two-and-a-half million years old. Leakey concluded that the creature, which walked upright and had a relatively large brain, was a direct ancestor of man. This meant that the species Homo Sapiens branched off from its ape cousins much further back in time than had previously been thought.

Ban on DDT

FOLLOWING EVIDENCE that DDT, which is used to spray crops against common pests, accumulates in the tissues of birds and animals and causes their nervous systems to malfunction (birds lose the nesting instinct and salmon forget to migrate), its use was banned in the USA in case similar damage should occur in humans. It continued to be exported to developing countries, where it was the cheapest way of controlling malaria. Some Third World delegates at the United Nations accused the industrialized world of operating a 'double standard'.

Last Flight to the Moon

THE AMERICAN *APOLLO 17* landed on the moon in December. The astronauts, who included the first civilian, a geologist, spent a record 75 hours on the surface collecting specimens. This was the last scheduled moon flight. From now onwards NASA planned to concentrate on launching unstaffed space craft to send back data about more distant planets.

War in the

The Middle East explodes

THE SIMMERING TENSION between Israel and her Arab neighbours exploded into full-scale war on 6 October, when Egypt and Syria launched a surprise attack. It began on the afternoon of Yom Kippur, the Day of Atonement, one of the holiest days in the Jewish calendar. Isreal was totally unprepared. Almost unopposed the Egyptian army, backed up by Russian-built surface to air missiles (SAMs), crossed the Suez Canal and advanced into Sinai. Syria overran the settlements on the Golan Heights and reached the shores of Lake Galilee.

In their baseness the aggressors are spreading lies to the effect that it was Israel who opened fire. But the responsibility for the renewal of the fighting and for the bloodshed lies with them alone. Our enemies had hoped to take Israel's citizens by surprise on the Day of Atonement, when so many are engaged in fasting and prayer in the synagogues...but we were not taken by surprise...We have no doubts as to our victory.
Part of a television and radio broadcast by the Israeli Prime Minister, Mrs Golda Meir, on the evening of 6 October.

The enemies of God have committed aggression on Muslim lands and desecrated our sanctuaries. It has become the duty of every Muslim to make every sacrifice to liberate Muslim territory from Zionist aggressors.
Part of the statement by Egyptian Muslim religious leaders declaring the war against Israel a 'Jihad' or holy war.

Early days of the Yom Kippur War: Egyptian tanks cross the Suez Canal into Israel.

Israel strikes back

AFTER TWO CHAOTIC DAYS Israel struck back. On the 9 October she bombed Damascus, the Syrian capital. By the 13 October she had gone over on to the offensive on the Golan Heights. The Syrians began to retreat. In the Sinai Egyptian and Israeli armies met head on in the biggest tank battle since the Second World War. Copying the German Blitzkrieg tactics of 1940, the Israelis punched a hole in the Egyptian line and crossed the Suez Canal, destroying the SAM missile sites on the way. They besieged the town of Suez and left 20,000 men of the Egyptian Third Army undefeated but trapped behind their lines.

World alert

BOTH SUPERPOWERS had meddled in Middle Eastern affairs from time to time and both supplied their favourite side with armaments. On 22 October President Nixon heard rumours that the Russians were about to send a military force to the aid of the Arabs. He put all American bases around the world on to 'Red Alert', and for a few hours it seemed as if the local war was about to flare up into a serious international crisis. Before the world even had time to be aware of it, however, the tension was diffused by a personal call from Nixon to Brezhnev on the 'Hot Line' – an important victory for the spirit of Detente.

Ceasefire

By the third week in November the fighting had reached stalemate. Both sides were exhausted. At Km 101 on the Cairo to Suez road the Israeli and Egyptian armies signed a ceasefire. A United Nations force was sent to supervise the truce. No ceasefire was yet signed with Syria.

Middle East

A new spirit of Realism?

THE WAR CHANGED MANY ATTITUDES. Israel's confidence that she could always beat the Arabs in battle was shaken. The superpowers had learned how dangerous local conflicts could be to world peace. For both sides the war had been costly in men and equipment. For the first time there were signs of a willingness to search for a peaceful settlement. In December, representatives from Israel, Egypt and Jordan (who did not fight in the war) met at Geneva, although nothing was actually achieved at this meeting.

The Palestinians protest

THE PALESTINIANS feared that a peace might be made that ignored their rights. They advertised their distrust of the Geneva meeting by refusing to attend and by tossing hand grenades into a Pan Am jet on the tarmac at Rome Airport in December, killing 30 passengers.

The lights go out

EVERYWHERE emergency conservation measures were hurried through. There were few Christmas lights in the streets of Western capitals that year. Thermostats were turned down in public buildings, speed limits were lowered. In Holland, Denmark and West Germany driving on Sundays was banned, creating some strange sights on Europe's usually busy roads. Everywhere plans were drawn up for petrol rationing. Price rises and the shortage of oil for industry caused secondary problems of unemployment and higher inflation.

About 1000 West German drivers ignored the Sunday driving ban today as Europe's most complex and most heavily-used road network gave over to cyclists, walkers and horse-riders. Police, who set up 40000 control points throughout the country, generally levied fines of DM.50 (£8) on the spot on motorists unable to produce an excuse. People obliged to work on Sundays and provided with a letter from their employer are exempt.

Traffic on the autobahns fell from the Sunday norm of 3000 an hour to only 20, say police. Nearly all garages were closed, and police reported a marked increase in the theft of petrol from parked cars.
Report in the *Daily Telegraph*, 8 December

The energy debate

BY THE NEW YEAR the OPEC states were persuaded that Western nations were doing their best to bring Israel to the conference table and eased the boycott. The worst of the crisis was over! But the West had been jolted into an awareness of just how fragile and open to blackmail their societies were. And there were even more serious implications. For the first time people began to think seriously about the world's resources and to realize that they were not limitless. The great energy debate had begun.

Oil crisis; Londoners collect petrol rations coupons from the Post Office in November. Rationing was never actually introduced in Britain, but was elsewhere in Europe.

The oil weapon

DURING THE WAR the Arab states discovered a new weapon more powerful than any military one. Countries belonging to OPEC (Organization of Petroleum Exporting Countries) announced that they would cut oil deliveries to western nations and Japan by 5 per cent each month until Israel agreed to return to her 1967 frontiers. At the same time the price of oil would be doubled. Overnight the West, with its profligate use of energy, realized how dependent it had become on 'black gold'. The face of OPEC's chairman, Sheikh Yamani of Saudi Arabia, became as familiar on the TV screens as those of Nixon and Brezhnev.

Ceasefire in Vietnam

ON 27 JANUARY a ceasefire was finally signed between the United States and North Vietnam and all US troops were withdrawn. The two Vietnams were left to find a 'political' solution to their differences. There was no guarantee that either of them would keep their promise not to use force, and no clever phrasing could disguise the fact that after ten years and over three million deaths the USA was leaving Vietnam in much the same divided and uncertain condition that she had found her. To an ecstatic welcome, American prisoners of war, some of whom had been in captivity since 1966, came home. Once the joy was over, many were to find readjustment to life in America very difficult.

Tears ran freely down the faces of thousands of Americans as they watched the return of their sick, wounded or lame comrades, who looked pale and shy but were smiling.

Some of the prisoners gave stiff salutes at the aircraft door, walked shakily down the gangway, and then in a sudden burst of confidence pulled out of their uniforms hundreds of homemade banners with slogans like 'God Bless America and Nixon'. **Others waved small American flags, their only prison souvenirs, drawn on pieces of white material.**

'We've been thinking of ice cream for years', said one.
From the *Daily Telegraph* 13 February

Fragile peace in South-east Asia; Henry Kissinger (front left) and Le Duc Tho of North Vietnam (pen in hand) initial the Vietnam ceasefire agreement in Paris.

Nixon's bad year

AFTER THE TRIUMPHS of 1972, 1973 was a bad year for President Nixon. In the Spring two young *Washington Post* reporters, Bob Woodward and Carl Bernstein, discovered that the Watergate break-in had been masterminded by men high up in the administration, who had afterwards tried to cover up their involvement. Maybe even the President himself had been part of the conspiracy. Judge Sirica, in charge of the Washington Court where the Watergate burglars were on trial, was equally suspicious. A Senate Investigating Committee was set up to get to the bottom of things. It came to light that Nixon routinely recorded all his White House conversations on tape, and a battle began to force him to hand them over as evidence. When he resisted, many Americans began to assume that he must be guilty. By the end of the year his popularity had plummeted and the future of his Presidency was in doubt. In a quite separate incident, which did Nixon's reputation no good, Vice-President Spiro Agnew resigned in October, facing charges of corruption and tax evasion dating from his days as Governor of Maryland. He was replaced by Gerald Ford.

Coup in Chile

FOR THREE YEARS the attempt by Allende to combine socialism and democracy had been undermined by middle class opposition and extremists in his own party. By 1973 Chile was on the verge of class war and economic collapse. In September the army took over in a violent coup. When the Presidential Palace was captured, Allende died, possibly by his own hand. The new military junta, led by General Augusto Pinochet, suspended democratic rights, ruthlessly repressed all dissent and persecuted supporters of the defeated government. Over 6000 of them were shut up for weeks in unspeakable conditions in the Santiago football stadium where the 1962 World Cup had been played. There were rumours that the CIA, disapproving of left-wing governments in South America, had financed the coup.

Figure from the past

LIKE HER NEIGHBOUR, Argentina faced rising inflation and unemployment and was plagued by urban terrorism. Juan Domingo Peron, who had been President until he had been overthrown in a military coup in 1955, was still idolized by the people, to whom he was a cult figure who would solve their problems overnight. In June he was allowed back into Argentina after 18 years of exile and, at the age of 78, won the Presidential elections. His wife, Isabel, was named as Vice-President. Whether he could overcome Argentina's formidable problems seemed doubtful.

Britain part of EEC

ALONG WITH Denmark and the Republic of Ireland, Britain was formally admitted to the EEC on 1 January. The 'Six' had now become the 'Nine'. Not all Britons approved and the Labour Party promised that if they came to power they would allow the people to decide in a referendum.

Cod war

WHEN ICELAND tried to ban foreign boats from fishing within fifty miles of her shores, she and Britain became embroiled in a mini-war in the North Atlantic, which was known as the Cod War. In the early summer there were several serious incidents between British fishing boats, the Royal Navy frigates sent to protect them and Icelandic patrol boats. Britain had the letter of the law on her side but many people thought she was acting ungenerously.

Bombs in London

HARRODS, Euston Station and Conservative Party Headquarters were among the targets when the IRA brought their bombing campaign to London in August. For a while, bombs, some genuine and some hoaxes, became a part of British life. People got used to evacuating buildings in a hurry.

Secret Police surround the Presidential Palace in Santiago during the overthrow of Allende.

Dark days in Britain: Londoners read the grim industrial news by candlelight.

The three day week

THE OIL CRISIS hit Britain doubly hard as it coincided with an energy crisis of her own – the climax to three and a half years growing tension between unions and government. In November the miners demanded a much bigger pay rise than they were entitled to under Phase 3 of the incomes policy, arguing that the dangerous nature of their work made them a 'special case'. An overtime ban began at a time when coal stocks were unusually low.

Faced with an acute energy shortage, the government declared a state of emergency. A month later it was announced that after Christmas electricity supplies to industry would be rationed to three days a week. Severe restrictions were also placed on lighting and heating in public buildings. Factories began to lay off workers, and shops and offices were plunged into dark and cold. Britain faced an uncertain 1974.

Veteran film-maker honoured

SINCE THE 1920s, Luis Bunuel had been making surrealistic, often grotesque films mocking the lifestyle of the middle classes and the values of the existing social order. Although considered by many to be a great film-maker, his work had won little public recognition and was banned in his native Spain. In 1973, however, his latest film, *The Discreet Charm of the Bourgeoisie*, won the Academy Award for the best foreign film of the year. Bunuel, who had always claimed that he would reject any 'establishment' honours that came his way, accepted the award. To refuse, he said, would look like a publicity stunt.

Television

IN THE UNITED STATES the surprise TV hit of the year was the broadcasts of the Senate Watergate hearings. When they first came on, viewers had complained about losing their favourite quiz shows and soap operas, but by the autumn the hearings had broken all the day-time ratings records and made the 78-year-old chairman, Senator Sam Ervin, into a star – a role which he entered into with gusto. Now people wrote in to complain about the return of baseball to the day-time screen.

Novels of 1973

The Honorary Consul, by Graham Greene.
The Black Prince, a subtle novel about human relationships, by Iris Murdoch.
The Siege of Krishnapur, by J.G. Farrell, a vivid reconstruction of an incident in the Indian mutiny. Winner of the Booker Prize.
Watership Down, by Richard Adams; first issued in paperback this year. The adventures of a group of rabbits that appealed to adults as much as children, perhaps because it awoke nostalgia for a vanished, rural world.

Some non-fiction books of 1973

The Gulag Archipelago, Part 1, the first non-fiction work by Alexander Solzhenitsyn; an account of life in Soviet labour camps, taken from interviews with 228 detainees. This book could not be published legally inside the Soviet Union.
Small is Beautiful, by E.F. Schumacher, which became the bible of those who believed that modern technology had done more harm than good.
I'm OK, You're OK, by Thomas A. Harris. How to improve your relationships and ability to communicate and therefore increase your personal happiness. This book was published in 1969 but only became a bestseller in the United States in 1973, as the cult of personal fitness took off.

Obituaries

TWO SPANIARDS whose work was banned in their own country but which had had a great effect on twentieth century art died in 1973. They were the cellist and composer, Pablo Casals (b.1876), and the artist, Pablo Picasso (b.1881). Both men had lived in exile since the Spanish civil war and both had recorded in their art some of the tragedies of the twentieth century.

Opera House

AUSTRALIANS hoped to put an end to their reputation of living in a cultural backwater when the Sydney Cultural Centre was opened by Queen Elizabeth. The centre, which had cost 100 million Australian dollars, 20 years and many disputes to build, contained an opera house, theatre, chamber music auditorium and facilities for film shows, exhibitions and conventions.

Sydney Opera House in its spectacular setting.

Sporting news

THE DUTCH SOCCER CLUB, Ajax, won the European Cup for the third year running. As another Dutch club, Feyernoord, had also won the trophy in 1970, Holland could claim to be one of the footballing giants of the early seventies.

In a dispute over who had the right to discipline players, members of the Association of Professional Tennis Players boycotted Wimbledon. With most of the big names absent, lesser players had a chance to shine. In the men's final Jan Kodes of Czechoslovakia beat Alex Metreveli of Russia. In the women's championship, where the stars did play, Billie-Jean King won her fifth title when she beat the up-and-coming Chris Evert.

The Kohoutek flop

IN MARCH a Czech astronomer, Lubomir Kohoutek, discovered a comet which he predicted would pass close to the sun at the end of December. As it was larger than most comets, it should make a spectacular display in the night sky. In fact, as far as the general public was concerned, the 'comet of the century' turned out to be the flop of the century. It was so shrouded in vapour that it was visible only as a tiny spot of light. The best view was had by astronauts in the American space station, Skylab, which had been launched earlier in the year. The Scientists were happy, however, as they were able to gather much information from comet Kohoutek about the origins of the solar system.

Drought in Africa

NEWS LEAKED OUT over the year of two disastrous droughts in Africa, affecting the Sahel region south of the Sahara and parts of Ethiopia. Between fifty and a hundred thousand people had already died. For reasons of national pride, most of the governments concerned had tried to cover the disaster up until it reached crisis proportions. Only at the end of 1973 did help begin arriving from wealthier nations.

Apart from the human suffering, there were ominous signs that the effects of the drought had been worsened by man's own activities. Geographers began to talk of creeping desertification, which would be hard to reverse and would permanently reduce the amount of land available in Africa for cultivation and grazing, making future famines even more likely.

The natural vegetation of the Sahel, a mixture of savannah and succulent trees resistant to droughts in an area of scarce and irregular rainfall, is capable of sustaining a rich natural fauna, including antelopes, giraffes and rhinoceros, forming a balanced ecological community... This balance has been replaced by a man-made one consisting of cattle, introduced and protected by man, for whom livestock ownership is a question of economic power and prestige. The cattle have, over the years, exhausted the grazing available and as a result caused erosion over wide areas, so that in effect the Sahara desert has been expanding southwards.

The problem has been aggravated by a human 'population explosion' during the last few years, resulting from a reduction in infant mortality.
Report in *National Geographic*, 12 November

Pioneer 10 Makes It

THE US *PIONEER 10*, on its way to Jupiter, reached the 175 million mile-thick (280 million km) asteroid belt in May. But on 3 December it burst through safely, to pass above Jupiter at a height of 81,000 miles and take the first-ever colour pictures of the giant planet. Eventually *Pioneer 10* would pass beyond the Solar System into interstellar space.

Space age rail travel

I rode yesterday on France's latest turbo-train – a bullet-shaped train powered by four aircraft gas turbine engines – at an average speed of 196 mph – 40 miles faster than British Rail plan to operate their Advanced Passenger train in 10 years time. The turbo-train travelled at speeds only ten miles less than the world record of 206 mph. For passengers its attractions are obvious, and it is also far quieter and smoother than today's trains travelling at half the speed....

French railways now confidently expect government approval for a £250 million investment in a new line between Paris and Lyons, so that a fleet of turbo-trains, which would cut the journey time between the two cities from four to two hours, can come into operation by 1980. Although the turbo-train is well ahead of Britain's APT in speed and stage of development, it is not so advanced a concept. The APT tilting mechanism will make it possible for the train to run on ordinary track, while the French train needs a specially-designed straight track.
Report in *The Times*, 16 November

Beyond science?

THE PUBLIC IMAGINATION was caught by the apparently psychic powers of a young Israeli, Uri Geller. Under the watchful eye of scientists, he performed experiments that seemed inexplicable to conventional science – bending forks and other metal objects from a distance and without physical force. Some scientists were convinced that they were seeing evidence of powers beyond their understanding, but others suspected fraud and remained sceptical.

Downfall of

The suspicions mount

AT THE BEGINNING of the year, President Nixon finally handed over *some* of the White House tapes to Judge Sirica's court, where it was discovered that some sections had been erased and others were too fuzzy to decipher. The President's secretary took the blame and testified in tears that she had made a 'terrible blunder'. She had pressed the wrong button on the recorder and accidently wiped out some of the recording. Few people believed her, and seven senior Nixon officials including John Erlichman, Bob Haldeman and former Attorney-General John Mitchell were soon indicted for conspiracy to obstruct the course of justice by tampering with vital evidence. Whether the President himself had been involved at any stage was not yet clear. On 6 February the House of Representatives began its own investigation into whether or not Nixon had done anything illegal enough to warrant impeachment (dismissal by Congress), – something no American President had been threatened with since 1868.

Damning evidence

IN MAY the House Impeachment committee discovered that the transcripts contained some conversations that were also on the first batch of tapes given to Judge Sirica in January. Using sophisticated play-back equipment, congressmen examined the tapes and were able to decipher some of the fuzzy sections. By this method they were able to discover that bits of conversations had been omitted from the transcript in just those places where Watergate had been discussed between Nixon and his men. The evidence was not conclusive, but it did strengthen suspicions that Nixon had been involved in the cover-up since its very earliest stages.

President – I don't give a — what happens. I want you all to stonewall it, let them plead the Fifth Amendment, cover-up or anything else, if it'll save it, save the plan. That's the whole point. On the other hand, uh, uh, I would prefer, as I said to you, that you do it the other way. And I would particularly prefer to do it that other way if it's going to come out that way anyway.

Part of a conversation between the President and Mr Mitchell on 22 March 1973, that was discovered on the tapes but did not appear on the transcript. From the House of Representatives Report.

Dirty tricks

ON 2 JULY the Senate Committee published the result of its eighteen-month long investigation. It revealed a catalogue of illegal acts and 'dirty tricks' by the Nixon administration stretching back to 1968. The President had taken illegal campaign contributions, authorized telephone-tapping, sold ambassadorships, lied to the press and organized a break-in at the office of Ellsberg's psychiatrist, in the hope that he might blacken the reputation of the man who leaked the Pentagon Papers. These were not just ordinary crimes but threatened the very nature of American democracy.

The Watergate affair reflects an alarming indifference by some in high public office to concepts of public responsibility and trust; indeed the conduct of the Watergate participants seems grounded in the belief that the end justifies the means, that the laws could be flaunted to keep the present administration in office. Unfortunately the belief that the law can be bent where expediency dictates was not restricted to a few campaign officials.

From the Senate Committee report, 18 July 1974

Nixon protests his innocence

IN APRIL Nixon made a determined attempt to clear his name. He handed over to the House a transcript, 7300 pages long, which he promised contained all the relevant conversations on the remaining White House tapes. A week later he went on television to defend his actions. He placed all the blame for the cover-up squarely on his subordinates. He claimed to have had no knowledge of the original break-in or of the cover-up. He explained his reluctance to hand over the tapes as due to the sensitive security material included.

The end draws near for Nixon (right); Charles Colson, once the President's assistant, testifies before the House Impeachment Committee that he heard Nixon authorize the illegal investigation into the private life of Danial Ellsberg.

a President

The last act

IT NO LONGER MATTERED that the evidence against Nixon was still not watertight enough to convict him in a court of law. The President's reputation was besmirched beyond repair. On 27 July the House of Representatives issued three articles of impeachment, accusing Nixon of the obstruction of justice during the Watergate investigations and a long history of violating the rights of citizens. On 5 August Nixon addressed the nation and in a round-about way, without ever actually admitting his guilt, confessed that he had deceived the people by witholding information. Two days later, three prominent Republican senators, who had been among his staunchest supporters, visited Nixon and told him that if it came to an impeachment vote in the Senate he could no longer rely even on the support of his own party. On 8 August Nixon resigned in disgrace, the first US President ever to do so. Gerald Ford was sworn in by Chief Justice Warren Burger the next day.

By taking this action, I hope I will have hastened the start of that process of healing which is so desperately needed by America.

I regret deeply any injuries that may have been done in the course of the events that lead to this decision. I would only say that if some of my judgements were wrong – and some were wrong – they were made in what I believed at the time to be the best interests of the nation.

From Nixon's resignation speech, 8 August

The aftermath

FOLLOWING HARD ON THE HEELS of the Pentagon Papers and the horrors of Vietnam, the long-drawn-out Watergate scandal was a great trauma for Americans and shook their faith in politicians. American self-confidence, which had been such a feature of the post-Second World War years, ebbed away. This was to leave its mark on the rest of the decade.

Defiant in defeat: Nixon says goodbye to White House staff after his resignation.

Crisis election

NEW YEAR 1974 saw Britain in the midst of the 3-Day Week. By the end of the first week in January 900,000 workers had been laid off and millions more were on short-time working. A political crisis soon followed. On 27 January miners' leader, Mick McGahey, made a speech in which he dared the government to send in troops to mine the coal. As sons of the working class, he claimed, most soldiers would join the miners to overthrow the hated Heath administration. Under the slogan 'Who rules Britain?', Heath called a general election, hoping that public opinion would reject the miners' case.

The troops are not anti-working class – many of them are miners' sons, sons of the working class. And not only will we gain them but we will also gain the support of sections of the Labour and Trade Union movements to bust Phase Three, to defeat the Tory government and put in a Labour government committed to left-wing, progressive policies.
Mick McGahey, 27 January

Mr McGahey has made it abundantly plain that he regards this dispute as a political matter. Those of us who have taken part in talks with the NUM have known this from the beginning. And of course he has made it quite plain over the weekend...that the point of what they are doing is not to get a wage settlement in accordance with Phase 3, or even out of Phase 3. Its purpose is to get rid of the elected government of the day...in order to get a left-wing government, and obviously he expects a left-wing government to toe the line as far as he is concerned.
From an interview with Mr Heath on *Panorama*, 27 January

Stalemate

THE RESULT WAS DEADLOCK. Neither Labour nor the Conservatives had a big enough majority to form a government on their own. In the end Harold Wilson managed to put together a minority Labour government. Within weeks the miners had been given the pay rise they wanted and had gone back to work. The immediate crisis was over. The Industrial Relations Bill was repealed.

Difficult times ahead for Britain

BRITAIN'S TROUBLES were far from over, however, for the new government faced the formidable problems of a 17% inflation rate, rising unemployment, low productivity and a weak pound. Wilson placed his hopes on an agreement negotiated with the TUC called the Social Contract. In return for a government undertaking to restrain prices and follow a left-wing policy, the unions would voluntarily restrain their pay demands and keep Labour in power. Wilson compared it favourably to Heath's 'authoritarian' attempt to control wages by law, but the fact remained that the Social Contract's success depended entirely on the goodwill of both sides.

In October Wilson called another election, the first time since 1910 that two had been held in less than a year. This time Labour won a narrow overall majority.

The Irish tragedy continues

AN ATTEMPT TO FIND a way out of the Irish quagmire foundered in the spring. A new system of government by which Catholics and Protestants would share power was rejected by extreme Protestants, who staged a general strike in protest. Within a week Belfast was paralysed – without electricity, gas or milk and bread deliveries. 'Power-sharing' was abandoned as unworkable in the present climate; Ulster continued to be ruled from London and the 'Troubles' went on. In June the death toll since 1969 reached 1000. In November a clutch of bombs planted in Birmingham pubs by the IRA killed 19 people on the same night and injured over a hundred.

Revolution in Ethiopia

IN FAMINE-TORN ETHIOPIA the 44-year reign of the Emperor Haile Selassie ended when he was overthrown in a military coup. Relatively bloodless at first, the revolution took a more violent turn when a quarrel among the officers brought the left-wing Colonel Mengistu out on top. In one night over 60 ex-ministers were shot, among them one of the old Emperor's grandsons. Haile Selassie's own life was spared but Ethiopia's politics moved inexorably leftwards. The Mengistu government dropped the old alliance with the United States and asked the Soviet Union for aid in putting down a rebellion in the province of Eritrea. The 'Horn of Africa' looked set to become a new world hot-spot.

Jubilant Portuguese celebrate the army takeover. It was to be two years before something like calm returned to the country.

Nationalist surge

ONE SURPRISE RESULT was the success of the Welsh and Scottish Nationalist Parties, that had up to now been regarded as something of a joke. The S.N.P. now had 11 seats and Plaid Cymru 3, and with such a narrow government majority could hope to wield considerable influence. A new factor had entered British politics.

Revolution in Portugal

ANOTHER APPARENTLY STABLE REGIME toppled in 1974 with surprising suddenness. After 42 years of dictatorship under Dr Salazar (1932-70) and Dr Caetano (1970-4), junior officers in the Portuguese army seized power in a bloodless coup and promised the return of democracy. The country went wild with joy, feting the young soldiers as heroes. Long-exiled politicians like the socialist leader Mario Soares came home. Independence was promised to the colonies of Guinea, Mozambique and Angola, which Portugal had hung on to long after other European states had given their's up.

By the autumn, however, power seemed to be slipping into the hands of left-wing officers in the Armed Forces Movement (MFA), who were backed by the Communists. By the end of the year the future of the fragile Portuguese democracy seemed very uncertain.

Civil war in Cyprus

SINCE THE RACIAL VIOLENCE of the 1960s, the mixed Greek and Turkish population of Cyprus had made some progress towards living together in peace. All this ended in the summer of 1974. An attempt by Greek Cypriot fanatics under Nikos Sampson to seize power and force through 'Enosis' (union with Greece) provoked Turkey into invading in defence of the Turkish Cypriots. The full force of a modern army was thrown against the peasant communities of a small island. Greek villages were bombed and over 100,000 refugees fled before the Turkish troops. Racial hatred flared up again, and both Greek and Turkish Cypriots committed atrocities. Thousands of tourists were hastily evacuated. The spectre of an all-out war between the NATO allies, Greece and Turkey, loomed ever nearer. In the middle of August the combined efforts of NATO and the United Nations brought about a ceasefire. The island was partitioned, giving Turkey the northern half. Over 100,000 Greek Cypriots were made permanently homeless.

The Greek colonels tumble

SUPPORT FOR THE ABORTIVE SAMPSON coup in Cyprus brought down the unpopular, seven-year dictatorship of the colonels in Greece and led to the restoration of democracy. Greece held her first free elections for ten years, political parties came out into the open and exiles like the actress Melina Mecouri and the composer Mikas Theodorakis came home.

Out!

CHANCELLOR BRANDT of West Germany after his personal adviser was found to be an East German spy.

Prime Minister Golda Meir of Israel, who resigned, worn out by the rows about who was responsible for Israel's unreadiness in 1973.

President Peron of Argentina, who died after only ten months in office. He was succeeded by his widow, Vice-President Isabel Peron.

Heiress Kidnapped

WHEN IT COULD SPARE TIME from the Watergate scandal, American attention was gripped by a bizarre kidnapping case. Patti Hearst, daughter of a newspaper millionaire, was seized by a group calling themselves the Symbionese Liberation Army. As her ransom, they demanded that millions of dollars worth of free food be distributed to the poor. Then instead of releasing their captive, they announced that she had decided to join her kidnappers and take the 'revolutionary' name of Tania. Whether her conversion was voluntary or coerced no one knew. She was later seen taking part in a bank raid in San Francisco.

The cinema revives

IN THE USA at least, the cinema underwent a revival in 1974. Audiences were up by 20 per cent and takings by 28 per cent. Most of this was due to a handful of big-budget 'disaster movies' like *The Poseidon Adventure* (which cost two million dollars to make and grossed 16 million at the box office), *Towering Inferno*, *Earthquake* and *Airport 75*. Although critics saw little artistic merit in these films and accused them of pandering to public taste for escapism in a gloomy year, they were relatively harmless. The same cannot be said for another box-office hit, *The Exorcist*, which dealt with a young girl possessed by devils. Doctors reported an increase in the number of people troubled by nightmares and one New York psychiatrist described it as an 'unacceptable mixture of violence, sex and evil'.

Exile for Solzhenitsyn

THE RUSSIAN AUTHOR Alexander Solzhenitsyn was deprived of his citizenship and deported from the Soviet Union. He eventually settled in the United States, where he rapidly became disillusioned with the nationalism and self-indulgence of the West.

Solzhenitsyn on his way into exile; he was to become a prophet of doom for the West as well as the East.

Sports News

IN SOCCER 1974 was a good year for the West Germans. Bayern Munich won the European Cup and in spite of being frequently criticized as a 'machine' which lacked sparkling individual skills, the national team won the World Cup, beating Holland 2-1 in the final. England, who failed to qualify for the finals, sacked their manager, Alf Ramsay, after 11 years. Britain gained her first world boxing champion since 1946 when John Conteh of Liverpool won the world light-heavyweight title. Young Americans dominated Wimbledon. Chris Evert (19) won the ladies singles, while Jimmy Connors (22) thrashed the veteran Ken Rosewall 6-1, 6-1, 6-4.

West Germany – champions! Captain Franz Beckenbauer (right) in the final against Holland, which Germany won 2–1. Football in the seventies tended to be dominated by well-drilled defences and was often not very exciting to watch.

The fight of the decade

ON 29 JANUARY the man who many regarded as the rightful world heavyweight boxing champion won back his title when Muhammad Ali beat Joe Frazier. Later in the year he defended his title against George Foreman in Kinshasa, in a match that had as much to do with show business as sport. The fight started at 4 am Kinshasa time, so that it coincided with late-night viewing in the USA and was relayed by satellite to cinemas around the world. The fight showed that Ali had lost none of his skill. For seven rounds he dodged about until Foreman was exhausted and then he sprang, knocking his tired opponent out.

A new Stoppard play

ONE OF THE MOST talked-about playwrights of the 1970s was Tom Stoppard. In 1974 his fourth full-length play *Travesties*, a farcical look at the birth of the Dada anti-art movement in Zurich in 1916, opened in London. Its underlying theme was the gap between the principles men profess to hold and the hard realities they come up against in real life. Much of the play's effectiveness came from its skilful word-play.

Other popular films of the year

Murder on the Orient Express based on an Agatha Christie novel, with an all-star cast.
Last Tango in Paris starring Marlon Brando, which faced obscenity charges in Britain.
Stardust, starring Adam Faith and David Essex. A saga of the self-destruction of a successful pop group.
The Great Gatsby, based on the novel by F. Scott Fitzgerald.
Mahler, directed by Ken Russell, a 'stream of consciousness' film with a background of Mahler's music.
The Sting, starring Paul Newman and Robert Redford.
Blazing Saddles, a spoof on the traditional western, directed by Mel Brookes.
The Godfather, Part II, which won the Best Film of the Year Award.

The pollution debate

THE DEBATE over the harm done to people and the environment by the indiscriminate use of technology went on. Scientists discovered that the ozone layer of the earth's atmosphere was being stripped away, possibly by the over-use of aerosol sprays, allowing larger quantities of ultra-violet rays to filter through to earth – causing an increased hazard of skin cancer. An attack on that indispensable part of modern life, the motor car, came in a series of reports that linked low-level brain damage in unborn and young children with high levels of lead from car exhausts in the air. Chronic lead-poisoning was also claimed to cause learning difficulties in school children and delinquency in teenagers.

India becomes a nuclear power

IN 1974 India exploded an atom bomb the size of that dropped on Hiroshima in the Rajasthan Desert, thus becoming the world's sixth nuclear power. While India claimed that the bomb was being developed for peaceful purposes like mining, many people feared a proliferation of nuclear weapons that would make the world even more unstable. Canada, who had been helping India build nuclear power stations, suspended all aid on these projects.

Chemical plant blows up

IN JUNE a chemical plant at Flixborough in North-east England exploded, killing 29 people and destroying surrounding villages. Many people questioned the priorities of a society that could allow so dangerous a factory to be built in a residential area.

. . . If an accident is possible, however small the probability, then it will happen somewhere, someday . . . This is not all we have to worry about. We are about to encounter a rise in the number of nuclear power stations, about whose intrinsic safety even qualified people have doubts. An explosion in one of these is, as we have seen, sooner or later inevitable, and will make Flixborough look like a birthday party.
From a letter to *The Times*, 7 June

Other worlds

PEOPLE WERE FASCINATED in 1974 by a unique opportunity given by the US Mariner and Pioneer space probes to take a look at other planets in the solar system. Venus was hidden by its permanent thick cloud cover, but the photographs of Mercury were detailed enough to pick out features no bigger than a sportsfield. Most exciting were Pioneer 10's pictures of Jupiter, whose atmosphere of ammonia, methane, liquid hydrogen and water was believed to be the same mixture that had existed on earth when life began four billion years ago. Scientists speculated that the orange tinge seen on most of the photographs might indicate the presence of organic chemicals, the building blocks of life.

Medical breakthrough

ULTRASOUND IS A TECHNIQUE by which the body is penetrated by high-frequency waves which bounce back to form a picture on a screen. Unlike X-rays, it does not seem to harm the human body in any way and can be used to detect deep-seated tumours and look at unborn children in the womb. The first ultrasound machines were used routinely in American hospitals in 1974 and have since become commonplace.

The dark side of technology; the devastation around Flixborough.

Dole queues lengthen in Britain.

The end of an era

SINCE THE 1950s the industrialized nations of the West (including Japan and the rapidly-growing Far Eastern economies) had assumed that their economies would go on growing and their standards of living rising indefinitely. This illusion was shattered in late 1974 and 1975 when the inflation that had been gathering pace since 1970 was joined by a falling demand for manufactured goods. Rising unemployment followed inevitably. Economists called this slow-down in world trade a 'recession'. It was only partly due to the oil crisis, for inflation had started long before 1973.

No solution in sight

THE PSYCHOLOGICAL SHOCK was all the greater because no one was quite certain how or why it had happened and how to get out of it. Attempts to stimulate the economy would lead to more inflation, while curbing inflation by strict controls of wages and credit would have serious short-term consequencies. The economy would slow down further and unemployment rise a long time before any effects were seen on the inflation rate. The result would be a period of stagnation *and* inflation, which the press dubbed 'stagflation'. As living standards fell, political problems were bound to follow. Germans remembered that an economic crisis had brought Hitler to power in the 1930s. Despite this, most Western governments opted for a cautious anti-inflation programme.

The poor get poorer

THE CRISIS in the developed world paled in comparison with the problems of under-developed Third World countries, who also had to pay high oil prices. A spin-off from the recession was a fall in demand, and therefore also in prices, for raw materials, which fell particularly heavily on countries like Zambia, Zaire and Malaysia, whose economies depended on the export of one or two staple commodities.

If the rich nations go on getting richer at the expense of the poor, the world must demand a change. And we do demand change. The only question at issue is whether the change comes by dialogue or confrontation.
From a speech by President Nyeree of Tanzania at the Royal Commonwealth Society in London.

Recession

The giants totter

SOME FAMOUS NAMES in the industrial world collapsed or came near to collapse in 1975. The Japanese textile giant, Kohjin, went bust, triggering off a chain of bankruptcies among smaller firms. The car industry was particularly badly hit. One worker in four was laid off in Detroit. Governments in France and Britain had to bail out Citroën and British Leyland with huge subsidies. The great steel companies, faced with a world glut of steel, shut down furnaces and laid off workers.

The USA, who had produced 132 million metric tons of steel in 1974, only produced 81 million in the first ten months of 1975, while Belgium cut her steel manufacture by half. Even Japan and West Germany were severely affected.

WORLD PRODUCTION OF CRUDE STEEL (In thousand metric tons)			
Country	1974	1st 10 months of 1975	Per cent change 1974/5
USA	132,000	81,660	−18.4
Japan	117,140	78,190	−11.6
Germany, West	53,230	31,200	−22.0
UK	22,500	15,010	−10.1
France	27,000	16,220	−18.6
Belgium	16,230	8,810	−29.1

Source – International Iron and Steel Institute, British Steel Corporation

After months of rumour and indecision, the supervisory board of Volkswagen, Europe's largest car manufacturer, met yesterday to decide on drastic rationalization plans put forward by the company's chief executive, Herr Toni Schumacher.

Herr Schumacher's proposals . . . are expected to result in another 10,000 workers being added to the country's unemployed in the near future as part of a longer-term scheme for cutting the workforce by 25,000 from its present total of 133,000.

Such proposals would cause a stir in any firm at a time when the unemployment rate is at a 16-year high, but the shock is all the greater when this happens in a company that has for so long been the symbol of German economic strength and stability.

The Financial Times, 15 April

New York goes bust

THE PROBLEMS OF NEW YORK went back far beyond 1975. During the past decade over ten per cent of its population and many businesses had moved out to the suburbs, shrinking the city's tax base. At the same time spending on welfare had rocketed. Nevertheless, when the city announced in October that it was almost bankrupt and would no longer be able to provide services or pay its employees, the shocking news seemed symbolic of the times. Reluctantly, President Ford agreed to give the city emergency credit, and immediate collapse was staved off.

The future looks uncertain

TOWARDS THE END OF THE YEAR there were signs that the worst of the recession was lifting, but the West's confidence in its future had been shattered. It seemed to many that the age of easy affluence had gone for ever and that life-styles would have to change with it.

The speed and violence of the breakdown of sustained growth and full employment has been traumatic. . . In many sectors we had run into the buffers of capacity limits. If this is a correct analysis it may not be possible to return to 5 per cent growth rates (which imply a doubling of output in 15 years) on which full employment has been based.

Few political leaders and few of their economic advisers have thought out the implications of this possibility. It could mean a 'natural' level of very high unemployment, because the present level of industrial capacity cannot provide enough jobs for everybody. . . This kind of unemployment may call for nothing less than the restructuring of society, with radical changes in habits attitudes, and expectations. There will have to be much retraining for new skills. There may even have to be planned sharing of what work there is to do and quite new emphasis on leisure and its desirability.

From an article by the economist, Harford Thomas in the *Britannica Year Book* for 1975, published in 1976

The dominoes fall

IN APRIL the North Vietnamese launched a sudden attack on the South, and within three weeks Southern resistance had collapsed. In the hours before Saigon fell, terrible scenes of panic took place at the US embassy as thousands of Vietnamese tried to squeeze on board American helicopters to be airlifted out. 130,000 eventually escaped to an uncertain future in whatever countries would take them in, but many more were left behind. The triumphant Communists renamed the city 'Ho Chi Minh City' after the first leader of North Vietnam and began a clean-up campaign against features of the 'American way of life' such as night clubs and prostitution. There were no immediate signs of reprisals. Two weeks earlier, on 17 April, the Cambodian communists, the Khmer Rouge, had seized power there with hardly a fight. The country was renamed Kampuchea and the 2½ million inhabitants of the capital, Phnom Penh, were driven out for 're-education' in the countryside. All communication with the outside world ceased.

The Americans turn their backs

AS THE ATTACK on South Vietnam got underway, President Ford appealed to Congress to send aid to the South and was refused. Many saw this as the end of an era that had begun in 1945 when the United States acted as the world's policeman against Communism.

Portugal in ferment

THE PORTUGUESE REVOLUTION staggered from crisis to crisis. When the first free elections to be held there for 50 years resulted in an overwhelming victory for moderate parties, the Communists, who had received only 12 per cent of the vote, refused to accept the result. Firms moved out, inflation shot up and tourists, a mainstay of the economy, stayed away. Then in November events took a new turn. An attempt by the MFA to take the country over completely was foiled by moderate army officers and MFA leader, Colonel Carvalho was sacked. Whether this change of course would be permanent remained to be seen.

The last days in Saigon: an American helicopter airlifts US citizens and other foreigners out of Saigon as the Communists move in.

Independence for Portuguese Africa

MOZAMBIQUE AND ANGOLA were given their independence after five hundred years of colonial rule. Power changed hands reasonably smoothly in Mozambique, where the Marxist FRELIMO under Samora Machel took over. In Angola civil war broke out between contending factions – The Communist MPLA and its rivals, the FNLA and UNITA. Nearly half a million white settlers fled back to Portugal, adding to that country's formidable economic problems. Foreign nations like Cuba and South Africa began to meddle. Although Angola was potentially one of Africa's richest states, her future seemed bleak.

Civil war in Lebanon

NICKNAMED THE 'Switzerland of the South', Lebanon had long been an oasis of stability in the war-torn Middle East, where Muslims and Christians had lived in relative harmony. Now arguments over the future of the 300,000 Palestinian refugees, whose presence had laid Lebanon open to Israeli raids, brought relationships to breaking point. Civil war broke out, in which 6000 people were killed, the economy destroyed and Beirut left in ruins.

Recession hits Britain hard

WITH HER LONG-STANDING PROBLEM of low productivity, Britain was as hard hit by the recession as any. With inflation hitting 24% (the highest in Europe), it was difficult to persuade the TUC to stick to their side of the Social Contract, and the Labour government floundered. Wilson threatened to fall back on the sort of compulsory incomes policy he had derided during the 1974 election. The unions threatened more industrial confrontation. Faced with seemingly insurmountable problems, many fell back on the miracle that North Sea oil was expected to work on the ailing economy once Britain became self-sufficient in 1980.

Woman at the top

IN FEBRUARY the Conservative Party held leadership elections. In a personal humiliation for Mr Heath, the winner was Margaret Thatcher, the first-ever woman to be elected as the leader of a major party in Britain. From a modest background (her father had been a shopkeeper), decisive and razor-sharp in argument, Mrs Thatcher believed that Britain's decline had begun as far back as 1945 when both major parties had accepted the ethos of the welfare state. Now a return to the traditional middle class values of self-reliance and entrepreneurship was needed. Mr Heath, whom she obviously despised, had had the right ideas but not the courage to follow them through in the teeth of union opposition.

In the desperate situation of Britain today our party needs the support of all who value the traditional ideals of Toryism; compassion and concern for the individual and his freedom; opposition to excessive state power; the right of the enterprising, the hardworking and the thrifty to succeed and reap the rewards of success and pass some of them on to their children; encouragement of that infinite diversity of choice that is an essential of freedom; the defence of widely distributed private property against the socialist state; the right of a man to work without oppression by either employer or trade union boss. There is a widespread feeling in the country that the Conservative Party has not defended these ideals toughly enough, so that Britain is set on a course towards inevitable socialist mediocrity. That course must not only be halted, it must be reversed.
Speech by Mrs Thatcher to her constituency party at Finchley, 30 January

Opponents of Britain's membership of the Common Market hold a press conference in the run-up to the referendum of May 1975, which finally decided the issue once and for all. On the far left is Barbara Castle, next to her the Conservative MP Enoch Powell, third from the right trade union leader Jack Jones and far right Michael Foot. Anti-Common Marketeers were a mixed bunch with many different motives.

Britain's future under debate

SERIOUS QUESTIONS about Britain's future came up and were only partly answered in 1975. Welsh and Scottish Nationalists demanded devolution or self-government for their regions, raising doubts as to whether the United Kingdom could long survive in its present shape. In May Britain's links with Europe were finally secured when her first-ever referendum produced a resounding 'yes' in favour of continued membership of the EEC. Opponents of the Common Market put up a vigorous campaign against it. Some of the arguments they used are listed opposite:

An Anti-Common Market Pamphlet
Arguments against membership included:
The threat to sovereignty i.e. the right to rule ourselves as we see fit.
It would cause a huge trade deficit.
Value Added Tax (VAT) was so complicated that the amount of paperwork involved would drive many small businesses into bankruptcy.
The Common Agricultural Policy meant that Britain's efficient farmers would pay to subsidize inefficient continental ones.
Britain's control over her North Sea oil would be put at risk.
The links with the Commonwealth would be weakened.
'Remember – you may never have the chance to decide this great issue again.
If you want a rich, secure future for the British people, a free and democratic society joined in friendship with all nations – but governing ourselves – Vote NO!'

Some milestones
Died
General Franco, dictator of Spain since 1939. He was succeeded by King Juan Carlos, young and untried.
Sheikh Mujibur Rahman, the 'Father of Bangladesh', in a military coup which overthrew his government.
Emperor Haile Selassie of Ethiopia, under house arrest in Addis Ababa.
Arrested
Patti Hearst in San Francisco. She was indicted on charges of armed robbery.

The cinema

1975 produced some good films from all around the world. Some of the most interesting were:

Distant Thunder, by the Indian director Satyajit Ray; an atmospheric picture of the 1943 Bengali famine.

Fear Eats the Soul, by Rainer Werner Fassbinder, an indictment of racial prejudice in West Germany, that was all the more timely in a year when rising unemployment was stirring up resentment towards immigrant workers.

Hearts and Minds, an examination of the effects of the Vietnamese War on both American and Vietnamese society.

One Flew over the Cuckoo's Nest, starring Jack Nicholson, which was to win five Oscars in 1976.

All the President's Men, the story of the first unravelling of the Watergate cover-up. Dustin Hoffman and Robert Redford played the two young reporters.

Jaws, the commercial hit of the year, which grossed 95 million dollars in five months. It made the reputation of a new young director, Steven Spielberg.

Television comes to South Africa

FOR YEARS the South African government had resisted the coming of television for fear that it would introduce subversive ideas from outsiders that would weaken white control. In 1975 a colour TV service was finally set up. It was strictly State-controlled and no programmes were to be allowed that would undermine 'the Christian values of South Africa', threaten the security of the State or 'foster revolutionary aims'.

Books of the year

SOME INTERESTING AND READABLE novels were published in 1975. Among them were:

A Division of the Spoils by Paul Scott, the last volume in his 'Raj Quartet', dealing with the last years of British India.

Heat and Dust, by Ruth Prawer Jhabvala, another novel set in India. It won the Booker Prize.

The History Man, by Malcolm Bradbury, a black comedy about university life in the early seventies.

Changing Places, by David Lodge.

Humboldt's Gift, the eighth novel by American Saul Bellow.

Europe's Heritage in danger

THE COUNCIL OF EUROPE (part of the EEC) named 1975 'European Architectural Heritage Year', to draw attention to the way in which historic buildings like the Coliseum in Rome or Canterbury Cathedral were being damaged by pollution and the vibration from traffic. This coincided with a growing public awareness of the damage that had already been done by the sixties fashion for demolishing old buildings and putting up new ones of concrete and glass. Some historic vistas like the view of St Paul's in London had all but disappeared behind skyscrapers.

Old sports stars and new

A 13 YEAR-OLD RUMANIAN, Nadya Comeneci, surprised everyone by winning all the gymnastics gold medals at the European championships in Norway. She had been training systemmatically since she was six years old. A black American, Arthur Ashe, beat bookmakers' odds of 25-1 to defeat Jimmy Connors in the Wimbledon men's final. Ashe took the first set in only 19 minutes. The women's final, on the other hand, was won again by Billie-Jean King, her sixth singles championship. Muhammad Ali successfully defended his world title four times, but Red Rum failed to become the first horse to win three consecutive Grand Nationals. He was beaten by L'Escargot. When Leeds United fans rioted after the European Cup final in Paris, which Leeds lost 2-0 to Bayern Munich, the French and German press coined the term 'English disease' for the increasing hooliganism of English fans abroad. Leeds were then banned from international competitions for four years. This was only the start of a disturbing problem.

Europe's heritage in danger: a publicity poster put out by the Dutch Ministry of the Environment showing the damage being done to ancient works of art by air pollution.

Link-up in space

ON 17 JULY an event took place in outer space that was more significant politically than technologically. 225 km above the earth and watched by millions of television viewers around the world, American *Apollo* and Soviet *Soyuz* craft docked. The captains, Thomas Stafford and Alexei Leonov, then shook hands in space. This was the last opportunity for an American to go into space until the launching of the reusable space shuttle, scheduled for 1979-80.

North Sea oil

ON 3 NOVEMBER at Dyce near Aberdeen Queen Elizabeth opened a valve that let the first oil from the British North Sea fields into a pipeline leading to the BP refinery at Grangemouth on the Firth of Forth. The pumping of oil from the stormy North Sea was indeed a technological feat to be proud of, but whether it would prove the panacea for Britain's economic ills remained to be seen.

The microchip culture comes of age

DAILY LIFE was quietly being transformed by the microchip revolution. Cheap electronic calculators and digital watches were becoming everyday items. More significantly, an 'information revolution' was now in full swing. Details stored on central 'data banks' could now be processed and called up cheaply and almost instantaneously. Among the new gadgets made possible by this were automatic cash-dispensers at banks, computerized library catalogues that made it possible to see at a glance whether a book was on the shelves or out on loan, and computerized pricing systems in shops. Police forces used computers to build up a national store of finger-print records. In some factories, such as the Fiat works in Turin, programmed robots replaced human labour on routine tasks. This revolution, however fascinating, had its critics, who feared that automation would bring massive unemployment and that data banks threatened the privacy of the individual.

A white paper to be published soon will foreshadow legislation to control the use of data banks for storing information about people. Mr Jenkins, the Home Secretary, is known to believe that people have the right to see what is held about them. But that right should now be absolute.

The growing use of computers to store information about a person's credit-worthiness and other personal details has led to widespread anxiety about possible misuse. For example, should the information be wrong, it could lead to injustice for the rest of a person's life if uncorrected.

From *The Times*, 24 March 1975

Britain's hope for the future: Energy Minister, Tony Benn, opens a valve that will let oil from the North Sea flow into the BP oil refinery on the Isle of Grain in the Thames estuary, June 1975.

The right to die

WHEN DOCTORS IN NEW JERSEY refused to turn off the respirator that was keeping Karen Ann Quinlan, who had irreversible brain damage, alive, her parents took the case to court, pleading that she had the right to die 'with grace and dignity'. The court refused the request but opened up a nation-wide debate over one of the ethical dilemmas of modern medicine. Now that medical science had the skill to sustain life indefinitely by artificial means, was it justified in doing so even when there was no hope of normal brain function returning?

1976 Southern Africa

Caught up in the Cold War

THE UNRESOLVED political and racial conflicts in Southern Africa, especially in Angola, Rhodesia and South Africa, reached a crisis point in 1976. These were not merely domestic quarrels, for both East and West regarded the area as one of great economic and strategic importance and were not reluctant to exploit the situation for their own ends. Southern Africa looked set to become embroiled in the cold war.

World hot spot – Angola

IN FEBRUARY, the left-wing MPLA, which had been helped by Soviet weapons and 11,000 Cuban troops sent by Fidel Castro, came out on top in the Angolan civil war and set up a government in Luanda, the capital. The United States refused to recognize the new regime. It was, argued President Ford, nothing but a Soviet puppet, for which Cuban involvement was just a front. The Russian goal, it was suspected, was a warm-water port on the west coast of Africa, which would make the Soviet Union an Atlantic naval power and a direct threat to the United States. President Ford and Secretary of State Kissinger begged Congress to vote massive military aid so that the MPLA's opponents could carry on the civil war. Congress refused. The memory of Vietnam was still too raw for that. At the same time, South African troops, who had intervened in force in 1975 in support of the pro-Western UNITA faction, withdrew. For a while it seemed as if Angola's civil war were over and she would be left to sort out her own future.

The Civil War goes on

IN FACT, Angola's suffering was far from over, for she was now the centre of cold war tensions. As the year moved on, the civil war revived in the rural areas. Arms to keep up the struggle against the regime in Luanda kept pouring into Angola; so too did foreign mercenaries, mainly from Portugal, Britain and Belgium, who were paid $900 a month to fight. It was clear that much of the money for this found its way into the country from South Africa and the USA, where the CIA had a long history of bypassing Congressional rulings. In a trial that caught the attention of the world, 13 mercenaries (10 British and 3 American) appeared in court in Luanda in July. Four were condemned to death and executed. The Cubans, whose departure had been promised in February, stayed on. Peace in Angola seemed as far away as ever and relations between the super-powers became strained.

Unrest flares up in South Africa

EVER SINCE the Sharpeville demonstrations of the 1960s, while apartheid tightened and the gap between black and white living standards widened, South Africa's black population had remained relatively quiet. While outsiders argued that an explosion must one day come, white South Africans complacently assumed that blacks were happy with their lot. In June this myth was shattered. A law had been passed making the white language of Afrikaans the medium of instruction in all black high schools, even for children whose native tongue it was not. Black patience with decades of humiliation snapped. In the township of Soweto, 20 miles from Johannesburg, high school students boycotted their classes and took to the streets under the slogan 'To hell with Afrikaans'. The unrest grew rapidly more serious and spread to other townships, causing widespread damage and bringing the black educational system to a halt. Shaken, white South Africa retaliated with overwhelming force. When the riots died down, 140 blacks were dead, many of them children, and thousands injured. The world's attention was once again turned to South Africa.

A threat to Detente

I am going to make it clear to my hosts that the United States will not accept Soviet intervention in other parts of the world. Continuation of such measures must lead to a deterioration of Soviet-American relations.

Henry Kissinger, before leaving for a visit to Moscow, 19 February

in Ferment

Unrest spreads

NOW THAT THE FUSE had been lit, South Africa's long-smouldering tensions exploded. Outbursts of unrest continued and few African children went to school that year. Even the usually-quiet coloured (mixed race) population of Cape Province, whose civil rights were being whittled away, came out on the streets in protest in August. Seventy died under police bullets. Most white South Africans went on refusing to see that anything was seriously wrong with their system. The chance of peaceful change in South Africa seemed increasingly remote.

Soweto schoolchildren protest against the impositon of Afrikaans in schools.

Some facts about South Africa

Soweto has about 100,000 houses, in which an average of six or seven persons live in up to four small rooms, and a large number of wood and tin shanties. Less than a quarter of the houses have electricity, perhaps half of them have cold running water, and 15 per cent have inside bathrooms. Soweto has 256 schools, a 3000-bed general hospital, an eye-disease hospital and 55,000 cars. 850,000 people live there and at least 120,000 of them commute every day to and from their places of work in Johannesburg. Expenditure per black school child was only 6% of that for a white child in 1974, and only one in 50 black children attended secondary school.
International Herald Tribune, June 1976

Deadlock in Rhodesia

THE 11-YEAR-LONG crisis in Southern Rhodesia came no nearer a solution. Now that independent Mozambique offered a safe haven for black opponents to Ian Smith's all-white regime, the guerilla war intensified. Life for whites in isolated rural areas became steadily more insecure and dangerous. The death toll since 1972 rose to over 2000. In an attempt to root out the problem at source, the Rhodesian army raided into Mozambique. In August, an attack on a refugee camp said to be harbouring guerillas resulted in over 300 civilian deaths. It did Southern Rhodesia's reputation abroad no good at all. By the end of the year the two countries were almost at open war and a new troublespot had opened in Africa.

The world intervenes

RHODESIA'S TROUBLES were not her's alone, for she had become the focus of attention for other nations as well. Neither South Africa nor the United States wanted an outright black victory there, especially one led by a left-wing guerilla like Robert Mugabe. Throughout the year, both countries put pressure on Smith to do a deal with the guerillas. In the end it came to nothing, for Smith would not surrender power without firm guarantees for the future of white Rhodesians in the new state and the black guerillas, who were also divided amongst themselves, would settle for nothing less than outright majority rule. The guerilla war went on.

For 86 years we have lived as semi-slaves in our own country. Now you suggest that we must pay the oppressor. We are not prepared to pay this. We are demanding independence without any conditions.
Robert Mugabe

It is essential that we should fight for something worthwhile; this can only be obtained when we negotiate from strength. Otherwise our white population will leave, and the overwhelming majority of our black do not want this to happen.
Ian Smith

No end in sight

BY THE END OF THE YEAR no end was in sight anywhere to Southern Africa's crisis. And with world interest in African affairs running high, there was always the chance that any of these quarrels might become a focus for serious world tension.

The Iberian peninsula comes in from the cold

AGAINST ALL THE ODDS, democracy returned to both Spain and Portugal in 1976, opening the way for them to return to the mainstream of European political life. In April, under the protection of the moderate wing of the army, new elections were held in Portugal. This time the verdict of the people was upheld. The moderate Socialist, Soares, became Prime Minister and Portugal returned to civilian rule. King Juan Carlos of Spain, written off by many as a nonentity, broke decisively with the tradition of General Franco and announced reforms that would convert Spain into a parliamentary democracy. Elections were scheduled for 1977 and political exiles, some of whom had lived abroad for 40 years, began returning home. Both countries announced that they would apply to join the EEC, and Spain joined NATO.

Power struggle in China

MAO ZEDONG AND ZHOU ENLAI both died in 1976. As always, it was difficult for outsiders to discover accurately what was going on, but it appeared that the year was taken up with a struggle for power among Mao's successors. By October the struggle seemed to be over. Mao's widow, Jiang Qing, and her supporters (the so-called Gang of Four) were arrested and accused of abuses of personal power. Hua Guofeng became Prime Minister and there were signs of a cultural thaw. Films and books that had been banned during the Cultural Revolution began to reappear.

America celebrates

THE FOURTH JULY 1976 was the bicentenary of the signing of the Declaration of Independence, the birthday of the United States. Celebrations were held in every city, town and village, and the ships of many nations sailed past the Statue of Liberty in salute. In the midst of all their problems, Americans were able to congratulate themselves that the world's first modern democracy had survived intact for 200 years.

An unknown becomes President

IN NOVEMBER Americans selected as President the Democrat Jimmy Carter, who had been almost unknown outside his native Georgia at the beginning of the year. After the Nixon years his promise to bring honesty back into government and morality into foreign policy seemed refreshing.

Argentina – the army takes over

FLOUNDERING under the weight of Argentina's political and economic problems, Isabel Peron was removed by a military coup in March. Rumours soon began filtering out of repression and brutality by the new military rulers.

Catastrophe at Seveso

IN JULY a serious non-nuclear accident occurred that gave the world a preview of the risks man was running with his environment. A cloud of the deadly chemical – dioxin – was accidentally released from a factory making fertilizers in Northern Italy. As it descended to ground level, birds fell out of the sky and domestic pets dropped dead. Humans developed symptoms of poisoning and horrific skin rashes. The area was evacuated and sealed off. Pregnant women were told that their unborn children might be deformed and were advised to have abortions. It was later revealed that the area around the plant was so contaminated that the local inhabitants might never be able to return. No one knew what the long-term effects on human health might be.

Opposition to nuclear power grows

IN THE AFTERMATH of the oil crisis the industrialized nations had speeded up plans to build nuclear power stations. Many people were far from happy about this. Experts might argue that the chances of a serious accident like a meltdown were remote, but if the unthinkable did happen, then the human and environmental consequences might be catastrophic. Mass demonstrations against proposed new stations were held in France, West Germany and the USA. Public disquiet had some effect. Building programmes were slowed down in Germany and the United States. Opposition to Sweden's nuclear power programme played an important part in the downfall of the Social Democrats, who had been in power since 1945. But in the end it was obvious that there were limits to the willingness of governments to bow to popular pressure. France ignored public opinion altogether and went ahead with plans to provide for 27% of her energy needs by nuclear power by 1985. The massive Soviet programme was unaffected.

The pound in trouble

ALL YEAR the pound had been falling in value on the international exchange markets. In October it collapsed to an all-time low of £1.56 against the dollar (until March 1976 the pound had never been worth less than two dollars). Cap in hand, the government was forced to ask the International Monetary Fund for a loan of 3·9 billion dollars, and rumours spread that the IMF had made a loan conditional on sweeping cuts in public expenditure. The rumours were confirmed when Chancellor Healey introduced them in a mini-budget in December, along with plans for the sort of compulsory incomes policy that had been so unpopular under Heath. The government was criticized from all sides. The Conservatives raged about Britain's humiliation and Labour MPs accused their own leadership of putting the interests of international bankers above the living standards of ordinary people – just like the Tories would have done.

The dark side of technology again: Italian policemen wearing protective clothing patrol the Seveso area after the chemical disaster there.

Drought hits Europe: a Welsh reservoir in the summer of 1976.

Changes at the top

BOTH THE Labour and Liberal Parties changed their leaders in 1976. Harold Wilson resigned in March by his own wish. He was succeeded as Prime Minister and Labour Party leader by Jim Callaghan.

The Liberal leader, Jeremy Thorpe, was pushed into resignation by rumours of shady financial dealings, and the allegations of a certain Norman Scott that he had had a homosexual relationship with Thorpe 17 years before. The truth of the matter remained murky, but to many the hounding of Thorpe by sections of the press proved that British society was still puritanical and hypocritical. David Steel took over the leadership.

Sections of the press have turned a series of allegations into a sustained witch-hunt and there is no indication that it will not continue. No man can effectively lead a party if the greater part of his time is to be devoted to answering allegations and to countering plots and intrigues.
From Jeremy Thorpe's resignation letter, 10 May

Drought hits Europe

IN NORTHERN EUROPE the spring and summer of 1976 were the hottest and driest in living memory. Everywhere grass turned brown, great cracks appeared in the ground and forest and heath were swept by fire. Farmers faced ruin. In parts of Britain water rationing was introduced. Just in time, however, the drought broke, bringing with it one of the wettest autumns ever recorded. The countryside blossomed green again.

Sport and the Arts

Scandal at the Tate

IN FEBRUARY *The Sunday Times* revealed that the Tate Gallery in London had purchased a sculpture by the American artist, Carl André, which it had never put on public display, and the gallery was forced to bring it out. It proved to be a rectangular arrangement of 120 firebricks. This comparatively trivial incident was blown up by the press into a major row, which was joined by all those who felt that the popular art of the sixties, which tried to create art out of everyday objects, had reached ridiculous extremes. The Tate was condemned for wasting 'public money', although, in fact, they had paid out only £600.

The South Bank Theatre opens

BRITAIN'S LONG-PROMISED National Theatre complex opened on the south bank of the Thames in London. The £16 million concrete structure housed three theatres including one (the Olivier Theatre) with a moveable stage that enabled actors to make eye-contact with the audience. The British theatre had been struggling financially for years, and complaints were voiced about the folly of spending so much money on a mere building. Artistic director, Peter Hall, did not agree:

This place is dangerously big. But it can't be blown up and it can't be turned into a bingo palace. The fact that it's here means that the government must take theatre seriously.

Montreal Olympics

BEFORE THE START OF THE GAMES, it seemed as if sporting feats would be overshadowed by politics. China threatened to boycott the competition if Taiwan was allowed to compete under the title 'Republic of China'. Arab and African nations actually did stay away in protest against the presence of New Zealand, who had played South Africa at rugby. In the end, there was plenty of excitement and high achievement, especially in the swimming, where there were 18 new world records. East Germans won all the women's gold medals for swimming bar one, and the United States all the men's except that won by David Wilkie of Britain in the 200m breaststroke. Nadya Comeneci gained a score of 39.75 in gymnastics – just one quarter of a mark short of perfect, and a new star – Ed Moses of the USA – broke the world record in the 400m hurdles. In the Winter Olympics held in Innsbruck John Curry had become the first Briton ever to win the men's figure-skating event.

Sporting Champions of 1976
European Cup
Bayern Munich
European Cup Winners Cup
RSC Anderlecht of Belgium
UEFA Cup
Liverpool
English League Champions
Liverpool (for a record ninth time)
FA Cup Winners
Southampton
Scottish League Champions
Glasgow Rangers
Scottish Cup Winners
Glasgow Rangers
Five Nations Tournaments
(rugby union)
Wales who won the Grand Slam
Wimbledon Men's Champion
Bjorn Borg
Wimbledon Ladies Champion
Chris Evert
World Series (baseball)
Cincinnati Reds
World Heavyweight Champion
Muhammad Ali, who successfully
defended his title three times
Grand Prix motor-racing Champion
James Hunt
British Open Golf Tournament
Johnny Miller

Some popular musicians and groups of 1976
Bruce Springsteen, American rock singer. He had had his first hit in 1975 with 'Born to Run'.
Queen, a rock group whose single 'Bohemian Rhapsody' topped the British charts for nine weeks over the New Year.
Elton John, perhaps the most consistently popular artist of the decade. His stage act, which included outlandish costumes and antics like jumping on the piano, probably had as much to do with his success as his music, half way between hard and soft rock, and his undoubtedly skilful piano playing. In 1976 he and Kiki Dee had a number 1 hit with 'Don't Go Breaking my Heart'.
Abba, who had hits with 'Fernando' and 'Dancing Queen' and made a movie that was a box office success – predictably.

Is there life on Mars?

AFTER SEVERAL unsuccessful attempts, the United States succeeded in landing a spacecraft by remote control on Mars. The technology involved was almost mind-boggling. The ship was equipped with a pick-up arm to scoop up soil samples and computer-run mini-labs to analyse them and send the results back to earth. When a section of the pick-up arm jammed, it was mended by radio signals beamed over 200 million miles. The pictures sent back by the automatic cameras were astounding in their clarity.

The early results caused great excitement among scientists when oxygen was found in the soil and photographs indicated that Mars had once been ravaged by floods, although there was now no liquid water on the surface and little oxygen in the atmosphere. Disappointment followed when no sign was found of the living microbes that might be expected to live in oxygenated soil. Scientists were forced to admit regretfully that there was no real sign of life on Mars.

High speed travel in the air

THE WORLD'S FIRST supersonic passenger aircraft made its first commercial flight in January. At exactly the same time, Concordes took off from London and Paris on route for Bahrain and Rio de Janeiro respectively. The 3500 miles to Bahrain were flown in 3 hours, 35 minutes. Thousands of onlookers thronged both airports to watch the take-off, but the drama of the occasion hid serious doubts about the plane's future. The Bahrain run did not attract enough passengers to cover its operating costs. It was banned from landing at New York's Kennedy Airport, although it had been given grudging permission to fly into Dulles Airport, Washington, for a trial period of 16 months. There were still plenty who criticized the plane on environmental grounds.

As Concorde's first passengers prepared to toast the dawn of supersonic flight in champagne yesterday, a tiny band of protestors clapped their hands over their ears in Mrs Ellen Mead's back garden less than half a mile away from the end of Heathrow's runway 28.

Noise monitors on her lawn registered 134 perceived decibels (PNdbs), the annoyance scale by which aircraft noise is measured, compared with the permitted maximum of 110 for subsonic aircraft and above the 125 PNdb threshold for pain in the ears.
From a report in *The Times*, 26 January

A technological wonder, but will it prove to be a commercial white elephant?

Doomwatch

BY 1976 the energy crisis and signs of environmental change were changing attitudes. Terms like 'ecology', 'conservation' were becoming part of the everyday vocabulary. Many people tried to make changes in their lifestyles in an effort to use up less of the world's non-renewable resources. They drove smaller cars – in the USA the gas-guzzlers of the 1960s went right out of fashion – took to bicycles, insulated their houses to save heating fuel, kept waste for recycling, and refused to use disposable or over-packaged products. There were those who argued, however, that such efforts amounted to nothing but tinkering with the problem and that sweeping changes would have to be made in the wasteful Western lifestyle if an ecological catastrophe were to be averted. Political parties dedicated to working for such change, like the Green Party in West Germany or the Ecology Party in Britain, sprung up, as well as environmental protection groups like Greenpeace and Friends of the Earth.

In the excitement over the unfolding of his scientific and technical powers, modern man has built a system of production that ravishes nature and a type of society that mutilates man.
From E.F. Schumacher, *Small is Beautiful* (1973)

A new disease

TWO HUNDRED AND EIGHT VISITORS to an American Legion conference in Philadelphia were struck down by a mystery illness three days after their return home. The victims suffered from a high fever, muscle weakness and severe lung congestion. Twenty nine of them died. Doctors were baffled, as no specific virus or bacteria could be found to account for the disease, which was given the name *Legionnaire's disease*. They just hoped that this outbreak was a fluke that would never occur again.

1977 Sadat goes to

New Government in Israel

IN MAY Prime Minister Rabin of Israel was forced to resign due to a scandal over his wife's investments. In the elections that followed the Likud Party under Menachem Begin came to power. Begin believed in the God-given right of Jews to settle in all the lands that had formed Biblical Israel ('Eretz Israel'). Under his leadership there seemed no chance of any compromise with the Palestinians and peace in the Middle East seemed further away than ever.

While an astonished world looks on, President Sadat of Egypt addresses the Knesset, November 1977.

Negotiations stall

THE TALKS that had begun at Geneva in December 1973 had made no progress. Over the summer the Americans continued their efforts to find a way out of the deadlock. In July Begin visited Washington, but resisted pressure from President Carter to meet the PLO at the conference table. Secretary of State Cyrus Vance, who toured the Middle East in August, came up against equal obstinacy from Arab leaders, who refused to recognize Israel's right to exist at all. At the same time Begin closed the doors on a solution further by encouraging Jewish settlement in the former Palestinian lands on the west bank of the River Jordan.

Sadat breaks the deadlock

ON 9 NOVEMBER, while opening a new session of the Egyptian parliament, President Sadat suddenly announced his willingness to break the deadlock by going to Jerusalem himself and meeting Begin face to face, thus lifting the 30-year old Arab refusal to step on Israeli soil. Two days later, on the Arabic channel of Israeli television, Begin extended an invitation. Whether Begin's offer was serious or not, Sadat accepted it. On 19 November the first Egyptian aeroplane ever to land in Israel touched down in Jerusalem to a warm welcome.

Jerusalem

President Sadat of Egypt landed at Ben Gurion Airport at 8 o'clock on Saturday evening for his first personal encounter with his enemies of four wars. A twenty one gun salute boomed out and an army band played the Egyptian and Israeli national anthems. . . President Katzir was first with a brisk handshake. Then came a beaming Mr Menachem Begin.

In the reception line were people Mr Sadat had previously only known as distant antagonists.

'Madame', he said to Mrs Golda Meir, the former Prime Minister, 'I've waited years for this moment'. The 79-year old grandmother smiled back and said, 'I've waited a long time to see you too'.

The Times, 21 November

The streets of Jerusalem were lined with cheering crowds. Mothers held up their babies to get a glimpse of the Egyptian President as the motorcade went past.

Mr Begin replies

MR BEGIN replied in Hebrew. He praised President Sadat's courage, for 'the flight time between Cairo and Jerusalem is short, but the distance between Cairo and Jerusalem was until last night almost endless', but held out no real hope of compromise on the Palestinian question. The land that Israel now occupied was her's by inalienable right and none of it would be given up.

The link between our people and this land is eternal. It arose in the earliest days of the history of humanity and was never altered. In this country we developed our civilization. We had our prophets here . . . This is where we became a people, here we established our kingdom. And when we were expelled from our land, when force was used against us, no matter how far we went from our land, we never forgot it even for one day.
From Mr Begin's speech before the Knesset, 20 November

The Arabs react

ON HIS RETURN TO CAIRO Sadat was greeted as a hero by Egyptians, but other Arab states condemned him as a traitor to the Palestinian cause. At the instigation of Colonel Gadaffi of Libya, six Arab nations, including Syria and the PLO, met in Tripoli on 2 December and formed an anti-Sadat front. Egypt promptly broke off diplomatic relations with the signatories. Arab unity was dead.

Before the Knesset

ON THE AFTERNOON of 20 November Sadat addressed the Knesset (the Israeli parliament). His speech, delivered in Arabic, was televised live to a spellbound audience around the world, who had never believed such an event was possible.

I tell you frankly and with complete sincerity that I took this decision after long thought; and I know quite well that it is a big gamble. But if almighty God has made it my destiny to assume responsibility for the people of Egypt, and to have a share in the responsibility for the destiny of the entire Arab people, then I think that the first duty dictated by this responsibility is that I must exhaust every possibility in order to stop the Arab peoples from enduring the sufferings of other horrendous, destructive wars of which only God knows the extent.

Firstly I did not come to you with a view to concluding a separate agreement between Egypt and Israel. . . The problem does not lie just between Egypt and Israel; moreover, no separate peace between Egypt and Israel could secure a lasting and just peace in the region as a whole . . . without a just solution to the Palestinian problem there could never be that durable, lasting peace the entire world is now trying to achieve.
From President Sadat's speech to the Knesset, 20 November

The aftermath

THE SPEECHES in the Knesset had shown that in practical terms the gulf between Egypt and Israel was still very wide, and it was wider still between Israel and other Arab states. At Christmas time Sadat and Begin met again, this time in Ismailia in Egypt. They emerged as personal friends but divided still by the issue of the Palestinian homeland. Nevertheless, few doubted that something very significant had taken place in November. Psychological barriers between peoples, that a few weeks before had seemed insurmountable, had cracked wide open. The bloody deadlock that had gripped the Middle East for 30 years was breaking.

President Carter's new course

IN HIS INAUGURAL SPEECH on 20 January President Carter of the United States promised that in future respect for human rights would be the cornerstone of America's foreign policy. In this he was reflecting the disgust many Americans felt at the way recent administrations had kept unsavoury dictators in power in South America and South-East Asia and lied to their own people over what was happening in Vietnam. Critics were quick to point out, however, that such high-mindedness had its dangers. The USSR might take it as a criticism of its own poor human rights record and Detente be put at risk. One of the first results of the new course was a treaty handing the Panama Canal zone – which the Americans had gained in 1903 by trickery and force – back to Panama.

A death in mysterious circumstances

TENSION CLIMBED HIGHER in South Africa when a black trade union leader, Steve Biko, was found dead in a police cell. The police claimed that he had died as the result of a hunger strike, but marks on his body indicated that he had been severely ill-treated. 15,000 attended his funeral in Soweto. Now it came to light that over 20 blacks had died in custody in mysterious circumstances that year.

South Africa in ferment: thousands of black South Africans give the Black Power salute at the funeral of Steve Biko.

Protest in Czechoslovakia

SINCE THE SOVIET INVASION of 1968, Czechoslovak society had become increasingly repressive. In January 1977, 242 well-known Czech citizens took the risk of publishing a signed declaration criticizing the government's violation of human rights. Many of the signatories were hounded by the authorities, losing their jobs or being subjected to long hours of interrogation at police stations. Some were imprisoned.

The right to freedom of self-expression is completely illusory. Tens of thousands of citizens are prevented from following their chosen profession because they hold views which are at variance with the official line. Deprived of the right of self-defence they are, in effect, victims of a kind of apartheid. Hundreds of thousands of other citizens are denied 'freedom from fear' since they are forced to live under the constant threat of losing their livelihood and liberty if they should freely express their opinions.
From Charter 77

West Germany's year of trial

WEST GERMAN SOCIETY was shaken up by a new wave of urban terrorism. On 5 September a gang calling themselves the Red Army Faction kidnapped Hans-Martin Schleyer (62), President of the German Employers Federation, in Cologne. The kidnappers demanded the release of imprisoned members of the Baader-Meinhof gang. For six weeks, while police mounted a massive search and public figures were afraid to go outside their homes without a bodyguard, a succession of photographs were sent to the press showing Schleyer's physical and mental deterioration under the pressure of repeated threats on his life. The stakes were stepped up on 13 October (confirming police suspicions that terrorists of different nationalities often worked together) when four Arabs hijacked a Lufthansa jet to Mogadishu in Somalia, killed the pilot and held its passengers and crew hostage against the release of the Baader-Meinhof prisoners. Just when public opinion had reached the point of hysteria over the government's apparent inactivity, German troops sprang a surprise raid on Mogadishu Airport and freed all the hostages unharmed. The next day Schleyer's body was found in the boot of a car near Mulhouse. He had been shot three times. Despite the outcome, the reputation of Chancellor Schmidt as a tough, decisive leader was much enhanced.

Silver Jubilee

THE MOST MEMORABLE British event of the year was the celebrations surrounding the 25th anniversary of the Queen's accession to the throne on 7 June 1952. At the Queen's own request as little money as possible was to be spent on pageantry, but the general impression was that most Britons greeted the occasion with genuine excitement and joy. On the evening of the 6th a chain of beacons was lit from one end of the country to the other. On the damp and chilly 7th, which was a public holiday, street parties and other outdoor festivities were held in every town and village. On 28 June the Royal Navy gathered in the Solent off Spithead for a grand review.

Never had London seen such an occasion since VE night. It began with a fire-work display over the Thames, the biggest the capital had ever seen. As it ended the crowd surged down the Mall towards Buckingham Palace. Buses were halted, cars unable to move and even the emergency services were stopped in the crush. Even the police joined

the revellers. Mounted policemen were heard joining in with snatches from 'Maybe it's because I'm a Londoner' and 'Jerusalem'.

As Big Ben struck midnight the Queen and Prince Philip appeared on the balcony of the Palace to the cheers of hundreds of thousands of well-wishers. There were cries of 'Ma'am, we want more' and 'We want the Queen', and the Queen came out for a second appearance.
The Times, 8 June

In the midst of the economic gloom, Britain celebrates: a Jubilee street party in the Elephant and Castle district of London.

A new face

ON THE DEATH of Anthony Crosland, Dr David Owen (35), MP for Devonport, became the youngest Foreign Secretary for 40 years.

The Government in trouble

CALLAGHAN'S stint as Prime Minister was not turning out to be an easy one. Although the economy took a turn for the better in 1977, the Labour government received little credit for this. Falling inflation, the improving balance of payments and rising pound made less impact than the long firemen's strike that began in November, or the scenes of fighting between police and trade unionists that took place outside the Grunwick printing works in North London during an industrial dispute there. There were signs that middle class voters, many of whom had voted Labour in the sixties and early seventies, were coming round as a block to Mrs Thatcher's view that Britain needed a revival of old-fashioned Tory values. The

government lost by-election after by-election to the Tories; its majority was dwindling away. At the same time splits appeared in the Labour Party itself. Left-wingers led by Tony Benn accused the leadership of governing like Tories and advocated a return to full-bloodied socialism.

The government solved its immediate problems by making a pact with the Liberals – the so-called 'Lib-lab Pact'. In return for Liberal support in the Commons, Labour would hasten through legislation on devolution. This bargain was unpopular with many Liberal MPs who feared that the party would lose its unique identity and get little in return, but the government survived for the moment.

Escapist fantasy?

GEORGE LUCAS'S space fantasy *Star Wars* beat all previous ratings records in the USA, Britain, Japan and Australia. The film combined sophisticated technology and breath-taking special effects with bits of magic and a fairy-tale type story about the confrontation between good and evil.

It is clear that the seventies audience is a different breed from its sixties counter-part. Disenchanted, today's movie goers want enchantment. Apathetic, they need the zap of Hollywood technology to keep them awake. Devoid of burning ideals, they crave the happy endings of old... With its dazzling special effects and mile-a-minute action, *Star Wars* takes the audience like a giant wave. It doesn't ask for your energy, it supplies its own. And for all the scientific accoutrements, *Star Wars* appeals directly to nostalgia. After all, the setting is not just far away but long ago. It is our childhood – and George Lucas's – that we are reliving on the screen. For the 'lost generation' of the seventies *Star Wars*, with its return to innocence and clear-cut morality, is the ideal movie.
From *Newsweek*'s review of 1977, 2 January 1978

The search for roots

THE TELEVISION SENSATION of the year in the United States was *Roots*, based on a book by black American, Alex Haley. Haley had traced his origins back to his maternal great-great-great-great grandfather, Kunte Kinte, who had been kidnapped from his village in Gambia by slave traders and shipped to America over two hundred years before. The confirmation that they had 'roots' in an authentic African culture of their own did much for the pride and self-confidence of American blacks.

The new protest singers: the Sex Pistols on stage.

Punk shocks

THE POP WORLD – AND SOCIETY in general – were shaken up by the emergence of Punk and 'New Wave' music. The Sex Pistols, astutely managed by Malcolm MacLaren, seemed to declare war on what complacency was left in British society by the shock tactics of their music, dress and remarks to the press – who had a field day denouncing them, and the punk fashion for spiky hair in green or orange, safety pins and slashed or torn clothes covered in zips, belts or buckles. In the Sex Pistols' wake came a new generation of artists: The Clash, the Jam and Elvis Costello from England, The Boomtown Rats (led by Bob Geldof) from Ireland, the Talking Heads, Devo, and Television from the US, and many others. The New Wave became an international phenomenon, often interpreted as a reaction against both the economic problems facing youth in western economies, and the increasing remoteness of the once-rebellious pop stars of the sixties – many of whom now only appeared at enormous and expensive concerts. Several British punk acts were interested in reggae and performed with West Indian musicians: the Clash's 'Police and Thieves' had been a hit for reggae artist Junior Murvin. The subsequent Rock Against Racism movement grew out of this connection.

I don't understand what people have got against us. All we're trying to do is to destroy everything.
Johnny Rotten, in an interview with the *New York Times*, August 1977

The King is dead

ELVIS PRESLEY, King of Rock and Roll, died on 16 August at the age of 42. He had been the idol of an era and sold over 400 million records. Although his career had reached its peak in the late 1950s and early 1960s and faded after that, thousands of weeping fans crowded into his home in Memphis, Tennessee, to view his body.

A British success at Wimbledon

FOR THE FIRST TIME since 1969 a British player won a Wimbledon championship. Having beaten the favourite, Chris Evert, in the semi-finals, Virginia Wade went on to beat Betty Stove of the Netherlands in the ladies final, despite dropping the first set and squandering a 3-0 lead in the second. A new star, John McEnroe (18) reached the men's semi-final.

Definitely not cricket

THE WORLD OF CRICKET was shaken up by the activities of an Australian businessman, Kerry Packer, who began recruiting players for a series of 'supertests' played on artificial pitches according to special 'Packer rules'. He offered such generous terms that he managed to recruit many of the world's top players including England captain, Tony Greig, and almost the entire West Indian and Australian test teams. The men in charge of English (and world) cricket accused Packer of trying to destroy the unique character of the game, and players who signed up with him were barred from playing in Test matches until 1979.

Blow-out in the North Sea

IN THE NORTH SEA OILFIELDS occurred a disaster that environmentalists had long feared. A pipe fractured during repairs, forcing out a fountain of oil that rose 60 feet above the drilling platform and in less than a week spewed out 30,000 tons of oil into the sea. Unable to control the situation themselves, the oil company called in the American trouble-shooter, Red Adair, who had dealt successfully with similar blow-outs in the Texas oilfields. After four unsuccessful attempts, the leak was plugged. In the end the environmental effects were less than had been feared. It was too early for the fish-spawning season, and a massive effort to spray the slick with detergent broke it up into minute droplets which dispersed naturally. There was no guarantee, however, that it would not happen again.

Into space and back again

ON 12 AUGUST the world's first reusable spacecraft, the *Enterprise* named after the ship in the popular TV series *Star Trek* was launched from the back of a Boeing 747 for its first solo flight, lasting two minutes. On this occasion the *Enterprise* did not leave the earth's atmosphere, but if things went according to plan it would be launched into space in March 1979. All available space on the first few flights was already booked by the Pentagon (for launching military satellites into orbit) and private firms making communications satellites. The charge for transporting a 100 km object was 3000 dollars. To hire the space shuttle for a whole flight would cost 19 million dollars.

Cheap flights across the Atlantic

THE CHEAPEST and most expensive ways to cross the Atlantic made news in 1977. After a lengthy legal battle, Concorde was given permission to fly into New York's JFK Airport, and its future seemed more promising. British businessman Freddie Laker had also had to spend many years in court before being given the go-ahead to set up a cut-price air service from London to New York. 'Skytrain' seats could not be booked in advance but only on a stand-by basis. People wanting to fly queued up at the airport just as if they were catching a bus or train. When the first Skytrain took off in September, a single ticket to New York cost £59, compared with £500 on Concorde. Despite a disappointing start, the service proved popular and profitable in its early years. Scheduled airlines were outraged, but forced to compete by dropping their own prices. Laker became something of a folk hero.

Twenty three nationalities came along to book tickets on this first flight from all strands of what I might call lower income earners. These people did not have the means to travel before Skytrain and obviously want to.
Freddie Laker in an interview on 26 September, the day the first Skytrain took off.

Sky train off at last: Freddie Laker celebrates the take-off of his first cut-price service to New York.

A Heroin epidemic?

ONE OF THE MAIN medical and social problems of the decade was the spread of hard drugs such as heroin and cocaine. European governments had once reassured themselves that this was a problem confined to the United States, but by the beginning of 1977 there were unmistakable signs that the epidemic had spread across the Atlantic. From that year onwards it was considered a major social problem. The amount of heroin seized in Western Europe had increased over 20 times between 1972 and 1976.

1978 New Directions

Where will China go now?

FOR OVER 20 YEARS Mao's brand of revolutionary idealism had stamped itself on China. During the Cultural Revolution in particular, revolutionary purity had taken precedence over everything else. Skilled jobs and places in higher education were given out on political grounds. Revolutionary committees supervised everything from private lives to the running of factories. Anyone thought to be lacking in revolutionary spirit was forced to do manual labour as a penance. Strict censorship was imposed, especially when Mao's wife, Jiang Qing was Minister of Culture. Until 1971 China had been almost cut off from the rest of the world. By the end, the economy was in a shambles and China had fallen a long way behind other countries in science and technology. In 1976, the Gang of Four, who claimed to be Mao's revolutionary heirs, had been ousted, but no one knew how willing or able China's new leaders were to set her on a new course.

Trial of the Gang of Four – actually a trial of ten 'leftists' known as the Jian Qing – Lin Biao clique.

The Four Modernizations

ON 25 FEBRUARY Premier Hua made a marathon 3½ hour speech to the National Peoples Congress. He accused the Gang of Four of ruining the economy with their meddling and went on to outline the 'Four Modernizations' – an accelerated development of industry, agriculture, defence and technology – that would put China on the road to becoming a 'modern socialist' nation by 1985. Production would be stimulated by giving workers bonuses and other incentives that had previously been dismissed as 'materialistic'. Foreign investment would be encouraged. The revolutionary committees would be banned from interfering in industry or education. Admission to universities would be made on the basis of school exam results rather than political loyalty, and children of former landlords and capitalists would no longer be automatically excluded. For the scientifically-gifted, 'key' schools would be set up – which Mao would have dismissed as 'elitist'.

in China

The rise of Deng Xiaoping

THESE NEW IDEAS had to be sold to the thousands of Chinese Communists to whom Mao's word was still sacred. The driving force behind this campaign emerged as Deputy Premier, Deng Xiaoping, who had been blacklisted as a 'renegade' and 'traitor' during the Cultural Revolution and made a political come-back during the early seventies. He could not yet attack Mao outright – just as Hua had had to blame economic backwardness on the Gang of Four rather than the dead leader – but many of his speeches that year were veiled criticisms of the Mao cult.

The wounded

DURING 1978 censorship was relaxed considerably and things that could not have been mentioned in the Mao era were freely discussed. Most remarkable was the appearance of novels and poems about the sufferings of the generation who had grown up under the Cultural Revolution. This became known as the 'literature of the wounded', after a novel by Lu Xinhua, which appeared in a Shanghai newspaper.

The story begins in the mid-1960s.
Although the heroine, Xiaohua, has broken all ties with her mother, she is still persecuted because of her mother's disgrace during the Cultural Revolution. She is forced to leave home and work in the countryside, where she falls in love with a fellow worker, Su Xiaolin. She breaks with him after reading his diary and learning that he has been warned by the local party that his friendship with her will harm his future. After the fall of the Gang of Four, her mother writes that her good name has been restored. Xiaohua returns to Shanghai for the first time in ten years to find her mother on her death-bed, waiting only to see her daughter. By her side is Su Xiaolin, also still waiting.
A summary of the plot of 'The Wounded' by Lu Xinhua

Democracy wall

IN DECEMBER foreigners in Beijing were astounded by the appearance of wall-posters criticizing the abitrary behaviour of some officials and demanding more genuine democracy and the removal of unpopular leaders. This experiment in free speech was probably instigated by Deng Xiaoping as part of his attack on the Mao cult, but it soon became genuinely spontaneous. Crowds marched in Beijing with banners praising democracy and mobbed foreign journalists with eager questions.

They asked questions that would have amounted to heresy – perhaps treason – a few months ago: 'Why can't the national economy catch up with the one in Taiwan?' 'How can the United States, a capitalist country only 200 years old, be the most developed in the world?' 'How could a handful of bad people run amok for ten years?'
From a report in *Newsweek*, 11 December

Chairman Mao was a man, not a god. The time has come to give him his real place. Only then will we be able to protect Mao's thought.

* * * * *

You can clamp down silence on the people again, but that won't solve anything.
2 extracts from Beijing wall-posters

New links

AFTER A FEW WEEKS the poster campaign was toned down, probably on the orders of Deng, who feared it might get out of hand. In order to modernize her economy China had to increase her trading links with the rest of the world. More Chinese delegations than ever before visited the West in 1978 and signed agreements to exchange goods and technical know-how. Fences were mended with the old enemy, Japan. The biggest breakthrough came right at the end of the year with the opening of full diplomatic relations with the United States, who made the great concession of ending her military support for Taiwan, another break with her role as the world's watchdog against communism.

The Coca Cola Company, long a symbol of American 'imperialism' to communists worldwide, announced yesterday that it will begin selling soft drinks in China next month and start building a bottling plant in Shanghai early in the New Year.
Report in the *Daily Telegraph*, 20 December

Into the future

NO ONE DOUBTED that great changes were afoot in China. Amidst all the excitement expressed by Western journalists, however, remained the fear that the changes might not go all that deep. Although the personalities at the top had changed, the Communist Party was still firmly in charge, and what the Party had given in terms of greater freedom it might just as easily take away again.

55

Carter's moment of triumph

AFTER THE EUPHORIA OF 1977 peace talks between Egypt and Israel had stalled over the Palestinian question. In September President Carter invited both Sadat and Begin to his country retreat at Camp David in Maryland and kept them there until an agreement had been thrashed out. In the 'Camp David Accords' they promised that a peace treaty between their two nations would be signed within three months and Israel would hand back most of the Sinai Desert seized in 1967. The Palestinian issue was fudged over, Israel merely agreeing to a vague principle that they had the right to play a part in determining their own future. This was hailed as a great triumph for Carter, for he had overcome Sadat's reluctance to make peace without a settlement of the Palestinian question, but it left many issues unsettled.

Detente goes sour

CARTER'S CLOSER RELATIONS with China and his emphasis on human rights, which included the reception of exiled Soviet dissidents at the White House, soured his relations with the Soviet Union. In July he threw down a direct challenge when he accused Russia of using Detente as a cover behind which they were extending their influence in Africa and building up armaments to an excessive level. In retaliation the Russians made so many difficulties that the signing of the SALT II Treaty, due at the end of the year, had to be postponed.

The year of three Popes

ON 6 AUGUST Pope Paul VI died of a heart attack. An Italian, Pope John Paul I, was elected to succeed. Within six weeks he too was dead. As his successor, the conclave of cardinals chose the first non-Italian Pope since 1527 – the Polish Cardinal Karol Wojtyla, who took the name John Paul II.

The new Pope steps out: the Polish John Paul II, the first non-Italian Pope for over 400 years, makes his first appearance on the balcony of St Peters in Rome. Few people realized at the time what a prominent world figure he was to become.

Terrorists strike in Italy

IN MARCH a former Italian Prime Minister, Aldo Moro, was kidnapped and killed by revolutionary terrorists calling themselves The Red Brigade (Brigata Rossa). This murder of a well-known public figure sent ripples of shock around the world. For a while, Italy, which also had serious economic problems like inflation and a collapsing currency, seemed on the verge of anarchy.

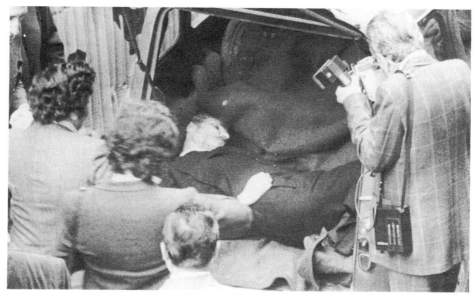

The body of Aldo Moro is discovered in the boot of a car. The kidnapping and murder of public figures was one of the outstanding features of the 1970s.

The war without end

THE CRUEL EFFECTS of the Vietnam war were not yet over for millions of South-East Asians. An ever-lengthening stream of refugees, unable to tolerate life under the Communist government, left the shores of Vietnam in any small boats they could find. Unknown thousands died. Those who made land safely in Hong Kong, Malaysia or the Philippines were often unwelcome in these already overcrowded places. Demands grew that wealthy Western governments had a moral obligation to take the refugees in. While governments wrangled, the boat people went on arriving.

At the same time news leaked out that between two and three million of Kampuchea's pre-1975 population of seven million had died in the aftermath of the Khmer Rouge takeover, when entire populations had been driven out of the cities into the countryside. Although this had been called 're-education', it was in fact a form of genocide designed to remove anyone who might be a threat to the new regime.

Britain's Winter of Discontent: health workers on strike.

The Shah totters

THE 37-YEAR-OLD regime of the Shah of Iran looked increasingly unstable during 1978. Disaffection among Muslim religious leaders, who had long accused the Shah of flouting the laws of Islam, was joined by protests from students and middle class politicians over the lack of democracy and the activities of the secret police (Savak). On the advice of his ally, the United States, the Shah made desperate last-minute efforts to democratize his government but nothing, it seemed, could stop the rot.

Election fever

BY THE SUMMER everyone was convinced that the Labour government could survive no longer and that a general election would have to be called before the end of the year.(In May the Liberals ended the Lib-lab Pact. Whatever high-sounding reasons David Steel gave for his action, it was generally believed that he had done it in order to give the party time to prepare to fight the election in their own right.) Jim Callaghan, however, held on doggedly. The government lost a number of votes in the Commons but refused to regard any of them as important enough to warrant resignation. As most people believed that the Tories were certain to win the next election, British politics in 1978 had a strange sense of unreality about them. Mrs Thatcher condemned the Callaghan administration as a 'broken-backed government that no longer has any authority at home or abroad'.

Industrial trouble looming in Britain

WITH THE INCREASING FLOW of North Sea oil, the economy continued to pick up. The value of the pound against the dollar rose and the annual rate of inflation fell below 8 per cent. At the same time union frustration with three years of pay restraint boiled over. When it was announced that under Phase 4 of the government's incomes policy pay rises would be restricted to five per cent – with exceptions to be made for the police, firemen and armed forces – there was widespread rebellion and a rash of strikes that disrupted daily life to an unprecedented degree. In October hospital engineering supervisors struck, closing 250 hospitals to new admissions and building the waiting lists up to 60,000. In December they were followed by local authority manual workers like dustmen and sewerage workers. *The Times* newspaper, which had already lost 13 million copies through industrial disputes that year, was suspended by its owners until further notice. With it went the *Sunday Times* and all the supplements.

Thorpe accused

ON 4 AUGUST Jeremy Thorpe, the former leader of the Liberal Party, and four others including an ex-party treasurer, were accused of conspiring to murder Norman Scott, the man whose claim to have had a homosexual relationship with Thorpe had ruined his political career. He was found not guilty the following year.

Discomania

THE HIT FILM of the year was *Saturday Night Fever* starring John Travolta, who rode high on the sudden appetite for new dance music – after several years of dancing to the same old records. Travolta followed up his success with *Grease* – a nostalgic look at growing up in the late 1950s.

The beat began in a make-believe bar in Brooklyn, and soon became the shout heard all around the world. Parisians mobbed cinemas that screened *La Fièvre du Samedi Soir* and Latins queued up for blocks to watch John Travolta and Olivia Newton-John relive the 1950s in the film they know as *Vaselina*. Television shows and T-shirts, best-selling albums and ubiquitous posters attested to the fact: 1978 was the year of discomania. And the discotheque itself – which had been relegated to the trend setters' dustbins along with hot pants and the twist – was suddenly the scene to make.
From an article in *Newsweek*, 2 January 1979

Sporting news

MUHAMMAD ALI lost his title to Leon Spinks, who like Ali himself had made his name as Olympic heavyweight champion. In September he won it back decisively, thus becoming the first man ever to win the title three times. Martina Navratilova, who had defected from Czechoslovakia three years before, won the Wimbledon Ladies title for the first time. Wales took the rugby world by storm, winning both the Triple Crown and the Grand Slam. The home team, Argentina, won the World Cup. The only British representatives, Scotland, had a miserable time – losing to Peru, drawing with Iran and failing to get beyond the first round. Willie Johnston was sent home early after failing a drugs test and banned for life from playing for Scotland.

Some films of 1978
Superman, starring Christopher Reeve. The latest big-budget spectacular.
Apocalypse Now, directed by Francis Ford Coppola which tried to show something of the true horror of the American experience in Vietnam.
Close Encounters of the Third Kind, directed by Steven Spielberg.
Midnight Express, a British film about drug smuggling.
An Unmarried Woman, starring Jill Clayburgh, about a divorced woman's struggle for independence.

The great marathon craze

LOOKING AFTER one's health – mental and physical – was a seventies obsession. Health food shops sprang up everywhere and joggers became common sights on the streets. An American bestseller of 1977 and 1978 was *The Complete Book of Running* by James Fixx. One feature of this was the marathon craze. Marathons had been run in big cities for years but only dedicated sportsmen had taken part. Now they became great public events. Over 15,000 ran in the 1978 New York marathon, three times as many as the year before and over six times as many as in 1976.

A new novel by an old master

AT THE AGE OF 73 Graham Greene published his twentieth novel – *The Human Factor*. Like many other Greene books, it dealt with the moral dilemma of a quite ordinary and unheroic individual caught up in a complex political situation – this time a British intelligence officer who once spied, in a small way, for the Russians.

Argentina win the World Cup: Captain Pasarella grasps the trophy after the 3–1 defeat of Holland, who were runners-up for the second time in succession.

Test tube baby born

THE WORLD'S FIRST baby conceived in a test tube was born in Oldham on 25 July. Because the mother's fallopian tubes were too blocked to let her conceive normally, the egg and sperm had been brought together outside the body and the resulting embryo replaced inside the womb. The baby, Louise Brown, was quite healthy and normal in every way. This breakthrough, which gave new hope to many infertile women, was the result of many years research by gynaecologist Patrick Steptoe and biologist Robert Edwards.

Smallpox eradicated

No case of smallpox has been found in the Horn of Africa – the last known reserve of the disease – for over a year, according to WHO officials. In Mogadishu, the Somali capital, today they expressed confidence that smallpox has been finally eradicated.

'We cannot be absolutely certain until two years have passed since the last case', another official said. Meanwhile, surveillance continues. A cash reward has been offered throughout the world for anyone reporting a case of smallpox but there have been no claimants.

'Once smallpox has been eradicated, it cannot reappear, as it can be contracted only through contact with a human carrier. There are no animal or insect carriers', WHO officials assert.

The Times, 27 October

The seas polluted again

THE WORLD'S worst-ever spillage from an oil tanker took place in March off the Brittany coast, when the *Amoco Cadiz* was holed and let out 220,000 tons of crude oil into the Channel. As well as damaging a beautiful stretch of coastline, the pollution threatened the local economy which depended on fishing and tourism. An outcry arose over the lax rules governing tanker safety, but no international agreement could be reached over new ones. With the narrow Channel now the world's busiest shipping lane, it seemed only a matter of time before another and even more devastating accident occurred.

A wonder drug?

ONE OF THE LESSONS of the seventies was that man, for all his intelligence and skills, was not all powerful. His control over the forces of human nature and the workings of the human body was limited. Nowhere was this shown more graphically than the battle to find a cure for cancer. Time and time again scientists had announced that they were on the verge of a breakthrough, only to find their hopes dashed. In 1978 it seemed as if the miracle might have been found in interferon. Most ordinary drugs used to fight cancer are dangerous poisons that destroy normal cells even as they destroy tumours. Interferon, a natural substance produced by the human body, seemed to be able to discriminate between healthy and cancerous cells and destroy selectively. But when trials began on cancer victims in the United States, they proved disappointing. The idea that man's ingenuity might produce a blanket, wonder-cure for cancer had to be shelved.

Some technological 'Firsts'

THE FIRST CAMERA with automatic focus – manufactured by the Konica Company of Japan. The user only had to place the object he was filming within a small square on the viewfinder and the focus was set at the press of a button.

Automatic washing machines programmed by microchips. These had far fewer wires and moving parts than ordinary automatics and broke down less often.

The use of laser beams to reveal finger-prints up to ten years old. This was invented in Canada and held out the hope of improved detection of crime.

Surrogate motherhood in cows. Eggs from the ovary of a cow were successfully transfered to the uterus of another and fertilized. It was hoped this would lead to improved stock breeding, as eggs from prize animals could now be frozen and then implanted in a recipient years later.

Nuclear go-ahead

INSPITE OF DOUBTS expressed by both ordinary people and experts, the Commons voted 224:80 in favour of opening the nuclear reprocessing plant at Windscale.

Mystery solved

FURTHER OUTBREAKS OF LEGIONNAIRES disease occurred in the USA in 1977. In 1978 scientists discovered that it was caused by a bacteria – *Legionella pneumophilia* – which thrived in moist places like water pipes and was often found in the heating, plumbing and air-conditioning systems of large public buildings like hotels and hospitals. It was very hard to eradicate.

1979 Revolution

The Shah departs

FACED WITH THE FINAL COLLAPSE of his authority, the Shah of Iran played his last desperate card. On 1 January he appointed one of his moderate middle class critics, Dr Bakhtiar, as Prime Minister and asked him to form a workable democratic government. He accepted only on condition that the Shah leave the country while things were worked out. On 16 January the Shah left for a 'holiday'. Few inside Iran really believed he would return. Who would finally take control of the oil-rich state – the politicians, the generals or the religious leaders – remained an open question.

Khomeini returns

ON 1 FEBRUARY the Ayatollah Ruhollah Khomeini flew in from Paris. (An ayatollah is a senior religious leader. The title means 'reflection of Allah'.) He had long been the most forthright critic of the Shah's rejection of traditional Islamic values and had spent the past 15 years in prison or exile. From the beginning there was no doubt that Khomeini had the charisma to dominate Iran.

When the chartered Air France 747 jetliner appeared in the pink haze of Teheran's morning sky, the rhythmic chant of 'Allahu akbar' – 'God is great' – spread from the airport throughout the city. The plane landed, and Ayatollah Khomeini, 78, set foot on Iranian soil for the first time in 14 years. Thanksgiving instantly turned to frenzy. Zealous young men swamped Khomeini's motorcade, while women sang: 'May every drop of martyr's blood turn into a tulip'.
From a report in *Newsweek*, 12 February

The new rulers of Iran: Ayatollah Khomeini (left) and his first Prime Minister, Dr Bazargan. Few doubted that Khomeini was the real power behind the scenes.

Islamic republic founded: soldiers and civilians demonstrate in favour of the new regime.

in Iran

Khomeini takes charge

WITHIN A MONTH Prime Minister Bakhtiar had been driven into exile and a new government under Khomeini's supporter, Dr Bazargan, installed. Although the Ayatollah took no official position himself and lived in semi-seclusion in the religious city of Qom, no one doubted that he was the real power behind the scene and had the last word on all important matters. The trial and execution of prominent supporters of the ex-Shah began.

American embassy stormed

THE MOST DRAMATIC EFFECT was on Iran's relations with the US. Khomeini reserved a special loathing for America, whom he denounced as the 'Great Satan'. Tension came to a head after the exiled Shah was admitted to the US for medical treatment on 22 October. On 4 November the American embassy in Teheran was stormed by thousands of students shouting 'Death to America'. Members of the embassy staff were taken hostage to be held against Iranian demands that the Shah be returned to stand trial. Although President Carter promptly froze Iranian assets in the US and banned the import of Iranian oil, there seemed to be little else Americans could do, short of an armed invasion, the consequences of which would be incalculable. By the end of the year as the world looked on in astonishment as the mighty Americans were humbled, the two nations remained locked in a battle of nerves.

Islamic Republic set up

AT THE END of March a referendum was held asking Iranians if they wanted the country to be ruled in future under strict Islamic law. The answer was an overwhelming 'yes'. Daily life in Iran began to change. Alcoholic drinks were forbidden even in private. In public places strict segregation of the sexes was enforced and women ordered to wear an all-enveloping garment, the chador. Public flogging was introduced for minor breaches of the moral code, and for serious crimes even more severe punishments were ordered, such as the stoning of women caught in adultery or the cutting off of the hands of thieves. Dissent was clamped down on by a new secret 'Islamic' police and press censorship reintroduced. Many Iranians who had fought to overthrow the Shah were horrified to find that they had opened the way for a new dictatorship.

We couldn't breathe under the Shah, and now we're suffocating. Many people are getting out.
An Iranian student who left the US to join the revolution in January

Those of us who lived through dictatorships have made up our minds. We simply can't have another dictatorship – Islamic or otherwise.
An Iranian university Professor – Reported in *Newsweek*, 6 August

The economy was disrupted and unemployment rose. Oil production fell. On their side, religious leaders argued that a disciplined Islamic life gave men and women a dignity that was lacking in the West, with its stress on personal pleasure and lax moral standards.

Spectator sport?

ON 1 FEBRUARY the *Daily Telegraph* summarized the possible cost of Khomeini to the West:

1. The loss of the world's second biggest oil importer will make a sharp rise in the price of oil inevitable.
2. The loss of a friendly power on the borders of the Soviet Union, from which the West could keep an eye on the Soviet military build-up.
3. The blow to American prestige. The impression that America is a 'paper tiger', which abandons old friends, could lead to some of her allies making agreements with the one super-power which still seems ready to behave like one, i.e. the Soviet Union.
4. Instability in the Persian Gulf and the narrow Straits of Hormuz will put the transport of the West's oil from other Gulf States at risk.
These are a few good reasons why we should not be content to view Iran's revolution as a kind of spectator sport.

Devolution dead

IN MARCH referendums held in Scotland and Wales failed to get the necessary 40 per cent vote in favour of the devolution bills that had been creeping through Parliament since 1974, and the idea was quietly dropped. Local nationalism, which had seemed so powerful a force in the mid seventies, had proved to be a nine-day wonder. The nationalist vote slumped badly in the general election.

The IRA strike again

THE LEVEL OF VIOLENCE in Northern Ireland had dropped over the past few years, although the underlying problem was no nearer a solution. The IRA suddenly struck out of the blue when they murdered the Queen's uncle, Lord Mountbatten, by placing a bomb in his boat while he was holidaying in Eire.

A tough year for Carter

PRESIDENT CARTER struggled through 1979. The embargo on Iranian oil led to a new but short-lived energy crisis in the summer. The dollar was weak. Inflation and unemployment remained stubbornly high. The President's attempt to pass an energy-saving programme was blocked by Congress. Many Americans blamed him for the humiliation they were suffering at the hands of Iran. By the end of the year he had acquired – perhaps unfairly – the image of an ineffectual President. The popularity of the ex-Governor of California, Ronald Reagan, who promised an economic revival and a strong foreign policy, rose correspondingly.

Russians invade Afghanistan

PROBABLY with Russian approval, a Communist government seized power in Afghanistan in 1978. For a year and a half it struggled unsuccessfully to win the support of the strongly Muslim population. Eventually the Russians lost patience. On Christmas Day 1979 they airlifted thousands of Soviet troops into the country, deposed the ineffectual President Amin and installed a Soviet puppet, Barbrak Kamal, in his place. The West, especially President Carter, was outraged. The last shreds of cordiality between Russia and America were torn apart. Detente was dead.

Settlement in Rhodesia

ONCE AGAIN Ian Smith and black guerilla leaders, Robert Mugabe and Joshua Nkomo, met to try to thrash out a solution to the long-running Rhodesian crisis. This time, at Lancaster House in London, under the chairmanship of Lord Carrington, they succeeded. Both sides compromised. Under British supervision free elections would be held, open to Rhodesians of all races. Whoever won the elections would then take the country, to be given back its African name of Zimbabwe, into independence. Whatever happened, white Rhodesians were guaranteed a set number of seats in parliament. One of the decade's thorniest problems had been solved at last.

New superstars

THE YEAR produced two unlikely superstars. The tiny Chinese leader, Deng Xiaoping, paid his first visit to the United States in January, where his charm and exhuberance won him instant popularity. Pope John Paul II made three spectacular, much-publicized tours – to Poland, Ireland and the United States. With his charm and wit, he had a charisma that was something quite new, but he soon proved himself to be completely conservative in key matters of doctrine like contraception, divorce and the position of women in the Catholic church.

The Sinai goes back

THE LONG-AWAITED peace treaty between Israel and Egypt was signed on 26 March. In November, Israel handed back the Sinai Desert and, in return, was given permission to use the Suez Canal. The first road between the two states was due to be opened in February 1980.

Overthrown in 1979

Idi Amin, dictator of Uganda since 1970, whose rule had become progressively more bloodthirsty and tyrannical – by the army of neighbouring Tanzania, who withdrew after organizing a new government.

General Somoza, long-time dictator of Nicaragua and ally of the United States – by left-wing guerillas, the Sandinistas.

Khmer Rouge regime, in Kampuchea – after an invasion by Vietnam, who, unlike the Tanzanians, did not withdraw.

Britain's winter of discontent

As PREDICTED, the rash of strikes in the public services snowballed in the New Year. The strikers, who included lorry drivers, ambulancemen, water and sewerage workers, dustmen, grave diggers and hospital staff, returned to normal working one by one in the spring, but not before the lives of millions of people had been disrupted. However good a case some of the lower-paid workers might have had, it was the chaos that stuck in people's minds. The Tories took full advantage of the opportunity to condemn the 'irresponsible' behaviour of unions who used their industrial muscle to win advantages for themselves at the expense of more vulnerable members of the population.

Britain's Winter of Discontent: the rubbish piles up in Leicester Square during the dustmen's strike in February.

Election '79

THE GENERAL ELECTION, which finally took place in May, was overshadowed by the winter's events. Predictably, the Tories won a comfortable majority of 43. One interesting feature was that the swing to the Conservatives was far greater in the South of England than in the North or in Scotland.

Given Mrs Thatcher's hostility towards the unions, many people expected a massive head-on collision that winter. Some even stocked up on candles and bottled gas – just in case. But by the end of the year it hadn't happened. Instead, a number of powerful unions, including the miners, had voted to accept modest pay offers rather than go on strike. What the significance of this was no one could be too sure, but it was clear that the mood of Mrs Thatcher's Britain was going to be very different from that of the 1970s.

Labour Party at odds

THE LABOUR PARTY, on the other hand, was tearing itself apart. The left argued that the election had been lost because party policies were not socialist enough. They set out to alter the way the party was run, so that the radicals would have more say. Roy Jenkins of Labour's right-wing hinted, however, that the time had come for a new party, more caring than the Tories but also free of the old Labour connection with socialism and the trade unions.

A triumphant Mrs Thatcher on the morning of her election victory, which made her Britain's first woman Prime Minister.

Sport and the Arts

A fairly typical year

IN THE CULTURAL FIELD there was nothing particularly distinctive about 1979. Many of the trends already established in the 1970s continued. Apart from *Amadeus*, Peter Shaffer's striking reconstruction of the death of the composer Mozart, the theatre produced little that was noteworthy. Some of the best productions were established favourites like the National Theatre's performance of Arthur Miller's *Death of a Salesman*. The cinema was kept afloat financially by more big-budget American productions, although the year also produced a crop of interesting and thoughtful films mirroring contemporary themes. In the pop world, new groups such as The Specials, Madness and The Selecter spearheaded a British vogue for West Indian 'Ska' and 'Bluebeat' music which was to carry over into 1980.

Facing up to the past

GERMANS had tended to push what happened inside their country during the Nazi period to the back of their minds. Those who lived through it did not want to talk about it, and the subject was hardly touched on in schools. In 1979 *Holocaust*, the American TV drama about the fate of a Jewish family in Nazi Germany, was shown on West German television. Thirteen million watched. When young Germans were asked about their reactions, the majority said that they were glad that at last they knew the truth about their country's past and were able to face up to it.

Sporting superstar: Bjorn Borg on the Centre Court on the way to his fourth successive Wimbledon singles title. His opponent was Roscoe Tanner of the USA.

> **Some films of 1979**
> *The Deer Hunter*, directed by Michael Cimino; a long and haunting look at the effects of the Vietnam War on a small Pennsylvania community.
> *Rocky II*, the second of the rags-to-riches boxing saga that made an idol out of Sylvester Stallone.
> *The China Syndrome*, starring Jane Fonda and Jack Lemmon; a topical tale of an attempt to cover-up an accident at a nuclear plant.
> *Manhattan*, a classic Woody Allen comedy.
> *The Chess Players*, another thoughtful and atmospheric production by Sanjayit Ray.
> *Man of Marble*, directed by Andrzej Wajda; set in contemporary Poland.

> **Some interesting books – fiction and non-fiction**
> *Sophie's Choice* by William Styron, which was later to be made into a film.
> *A Dry White Season* by André Brink; a novel about relations between black and white in South Africa.
> *A Bend in the River* by V.S. Naipaul; set in an imaginary West African state after independence.
> *The Right Stuff* by Tom Wolfe; the story of the first American astronauts.
> *A Distant Mirror* by Barbara Tuchman; a vivid picture of the fourteenth century.

Sporting news

NOTTINGHAM FOREST won the European Cup by beating Malmo of Sweden 1-0. This was the third year running that the trophy had gone to a British team (Liverpool had won it in 1977 and 1978). It puzzled many that British clubs did so well in international competitions, while the national sides had done so badly since 1970.

The Swede Bjorn Borg won the men's singles at Wimbledon for the

fourth successive year. He was to win again, for the last time, in 1980. Martina Navratilova won the women's event again. Mohammed Ali retired after a truly remarkable career. He was feeling his age and did not want to 'kill myself training to go 15 rounds'. Two new stars emerged. In the summer the British athlete, Sebastian Coe, broke the world 800m, 1500m and 1 mile records within a period of 42 days. The surprise winner of the British Open Golf championship was Severiano Ballesteros from Spain. At 22, he was the youngest player to win in modern times and the first from the continent of Europe since 1907.

Only a year after the first £500,000 transfer fee had been paid in Britain, Trevor Francis became the country's first £1 million player, when Nottingham Forest paid that much to Birmingham City for him. Many people feared that a handful of wealthy clubs might soon corner all the best players and the English tradition of having a professional football club in most fair-sized towns be lost for ever.

What will the world of the eighties be like?

IN ITS LAST EDITION for 1979 a Sunday newspaper ran a series of predictions about what the world of the 1980s would be like. A typically 'seventies' pessimism about the future was there but was less prominent than might have been the case only a year or so before. Alongside warnings about pollution and depleting energy sources was a new optimism that man's ingenuity would find a way around these problems. And much space was given to visions of a brave new world of high-tech, in which daily life would be transformed by the computer revolution. Which vision would prove to be most accurate remained to be seen.

Shuttle postponed

PROBLEMS with heat insulation delayed the first orbital flight of the American space shuttle until 1980.

Information revolution arrives

A WHOLE-PAGE spread of *The Sunday Times* was devoted to the wonders of teletext, which was 'far more than just another consumer product, it could be a development as significant as the invention of the telephone or the television.' Teletext enabled the customer to call up information from a central computer, which would be displayed on a screen in his home. The TV companies had already introduced their own version of this – Ceefax and Oracle – but the service it could offer was limited. According to the newspaper, the thing of the future was Prestel, a British invention, by which two-way communication could be established with the central commuter via a keyboard, display screen and specially-adapted telephone. Already available in London, it was due to become a nationwide service in 1980. There was no end to what it could do – from working out household budgets to supplying the contents of that day's newspaper on a screen.

A couple spot a holiday advert beamed on their screen by a commercial company. They like the look of it but want to consider alternatives, so, with a push-button selector, they summon up other adverts from a central data bank, which also provides prices etc.

The couple now use the system to calculate what they can afford (the computer has their financial standing on file). Having picked the holiday they want they insert a credit card into their screen to book the holiday and pay the deposit. The monitor prints out a confirmation sheet.
Sunday Times, 30 December

Millions of people would be able to work from home without the daily grind of travelling to an office, and chores like shopping and banking could be done without ever leaving the house. To some people such a vision seemed more like a nightmare than a dream.

A narrow escape

THE OTHER SIDE of man's technological ingenuity was seen in Pennsylvania in March, when the one-in-five billion chance nuclear catastrophe almost happened. A reactor at the Three Mile Island plant overheated, allowing radiation to leak out through the ventilation system. For a while a melt-down seemed possible. Thousands of people were evacuated from their homes. In the end the leak was sealed without anyone being hurt, although no one knew what long-term damage might have been done by radiation. The investigation into the causes of the accident discovered that a minor technical malfunction had been made worse by human error, which backed up those who argued that human beings were just too fallible to be trusted with nuclear power. At the same time President Carter warned Americans that they didn't have the luxury of giving up nuclear energy altogether.

Medical breakthrough

A NEW INVENTION – which made little public impact, but promised to improve the lives of thousands of chronically ill people who had to take regular doses of hormones or painkillers – was the micro-electric syringe driver. An ordinary disposal syringe was attached to a battery-powered device, small enough to fit into a shoulder holster. Small quantities of a liquid drug were then pumped into the body at regular intervals for up to 55 hours. Work was going ahead on a model that could be used by diabetics as an alternative to insulin injections.

Time Chart

World News	Sport and the Arts	Science and Technology
1970 (May) US invasion of Cambodia. (June) Conservatives win British general election; Edward Heath becomes Prime Minister. (July) Tokyo and New York smogs. (September) Five planes hijacked by Palestinian guerillas. Jordanian civil war. Election of Allende as President of Chile. Death of President Nasser of Egypt; succession of President Sadat. (October) Death of Laporte. (November) Demonstration at Miss World contest. (December) Treaty between Poland and West Germany.	(June) World Cup begins in Mexico. (July) *Oh! Calcutta* opens in London. (September) Death of Jochen Rindt. (October) Solzhenitsyn awarded Nobel Prize for literature.	(April) *Apollo 13* mission. (June) Discovery of Ekofisk oil field.
1971 (January) Postmen's strike begins in Britain. (February) Decimalization in Britain. (June) Pentagon Papers published in *The New York Times*. (July) Kissinger visit to Beijing; visit of President Nixon arranged. (August) Internment introduced in Ulster. (October) China admitted to United Nations. House of Commons approves Britain's entry to EEC. (December) War between India and Pakistan.	(April) American table-tennis team visit the People's Republic of China. (June) Evonne Goolagong wins Ladies Singles at Wimbledon.	(May) Test flight of Concorde. (29 June) Three Cosmonauts die aboard Soviet Soyuz space station.
1972 (January) Creation of Bangladesh. Bloody Sunday in Northern Ireland. Miners' strike in Britain. (February) Nixon visit to Beijing. (March) Direct rule in Northern Ireland. (April) Berlin Wall opened for family visits. (May) Nixon visit to Soviet Union. SALT II signed. (June) Arrest of leaders of Baader-Meinhof gang in West Germany.	(March) Tutankhamun exhibition opens in London. (July) *Ms.* begins publication. David Bowie releases *Ziggy Stardust* LP. (August) Fischer–Spassky chess tournament. (September) Munich Olympics: murder of Israeli athletes. (December) Death of baseball star Roberto Clemente.	(June) BEA Trident crashes over Staines.
1973 (January) Britain, Denmark and Eire admitted to EEC. Vietnam ceasefire; US withdrawal. (April) First shots fired in Cod War. (August) IRA bombing campaign in London. (September) Military coup in Chile. (October) Yom Kippur war begins. (November) Ceasefire between Israel and Egypt. State of Emergency in Britain. (December) Middle East peace talks begin in Geneva. Rome airport massacre.	(April) Oscar for Bunuel, Spanish film director. (October) Sydney Cultural Centre opened.	(December) Oil Crisis. Ban on Sunday driving in W. Germany, Sweden and Holland. Comet Kohoutek seen in night sky.
1974 (February) General election in Britain. (March) Labour government in Britain. (April) Revolution in Portugal. (May) Resignation of Chancellor Brandt of West Germany. (July) Senate Watergate Investigation committee reports. US House of Representatives begin impeachment proceedings against Nixon. Civil war in Cyprus. Fall of colonels regime in Greece. (August) Resignation of Nixon. Gerald Ford becomes President. (September) Emperor Haile Selassie of Ethiopia deposed.	(January) Muhammad Ali regains world heavyweight boxing championship. (February) Solzhenitsyn goes into exile in the West. (June) World Cup finals begin in West Germany. (October) Muhammad Ali fights George Foreman in Kinshasa.	(May) India explodes first atom bomb. (June) Flixborough disaster.

Time Chart

World News	Sport and the Arts	Science and Technology

1975

(February) Margaret Thatcher becomes leader of Conservative Party.
(April) Volkswagen workers laid off.
Cambodia and South Vietnam fall to Communists.
(May) EEC referendum in Britain.
(June) Mozambique becomes independent.
(August) Military coup in Bangladesh; death of Sheikh Mujibur Rahman.
Death of Haile Selassie.
(September) Civil war in Lebanon.
(November) Angola becomes independent; civil war begins.
Death of Franco in Spain.

(May) Television service begins in South Africa.
Leeds United fans riot in Paris at European Cup final.
(June) First Cricket World Cup held in England.
(July) *Jaws* released.

(15 July) Joint US/Soviet space mission launched.
(November) First oil pumped ashore from British section of North Sea.

1976

(January) Death of Zhou Enlai.
(March) Resignation of Wilson in Britain; Callaghan becomes Prime Minister.
(April) Democratic elections in Portugal; Soares become Prime Minister.
(June) Soweto riots.
(July) Bicentenary of USA.
Entebbe hijacking.
(September) Death of Mao Zedong.
(October) Sterling crisis.
Gang of Four arrested in China.
(November) Election of Carter as US President.

(March) Opening of South Bank theatre complex in London.
(July) Montreal Olympics.
(November) James Hunt becomes motor racing's World Champion at the age of 26.

(January) First commercial flight of Concorde.
(July) Seveso disaster.
(21 July) *Viking 1* sends first colour pictures of the surface of Mars.
(September) British Royal Commission on Environmental Damage advises against the further development of nuclear power.

1977

(January) President Carter's inauguration speech.
Charter 77 published in Czechoslovakia.
(March) Lib-lab pact negotiated in Britain.
(May) Begin becomes Israeli Prime Minister.
(June) Silver Jubilee in Britain.
Death of Biko in South Africa.
(October) Mogadishu hijacking.
(November) Sadat's visit to Jerusalem.

(June) Sex Pistol's 'God Save the Queen' banned by BBC. It tops the non-BBC charts during the Jubilee.
(August) Death of Elvis Presley.
England regain the Ashes from Australia at cricket.

(April) North Sea oil blow-out.
(September) Skytrain service to New York begins.

1978

(February) Premier Hua announces Four Modernizations in China.
(March) Kidnapping of Aldo Moro.
Amoco Cadiz disaster.
(May) Death of Moro.
Death of Pope Paul VI.
(September) Camp David Accords.
Election of Pope John Paul II.
(November) Strikes in public services begin in Britain.
(December) Democracy Wall in China.
Diplomatic relations opened between USA and China.

(June) World Cup finals open in Argentina.
(September) Muhammad Ali regains world heavyweight title for third time.
(November) *The Times* suspends publication until further notice.

(July) World's first test tube baby born.
(October) WHO announces elimination of smallpox.

1979

(January) Abdication of Shah of Iran.
Vietnamese depose Pol Pot regime in Kampuchea.
(March) Iran becomes Islamic Republic.
Peace treaty between Egypt and Israel.
(April) President Amin of Uganda deposed.
(May) Conservative government elected in Britain.
(June) Pope's visit to Poland.
Overthrow of General Somoza in Nicaragua.
(August) Murder of Earl Mountbatten.
(November) Occupation of US embassy in Teheran.
Lancaster House talks end UDI in Southern Rhodesia.
Israel hands Sinai Desert back to Egypt.
(December) Russian invasion of Afghanistan.

(May) Nottingham Forest win European Cup. Third win in a row for British clubs.
(July) Sebastian Coe breaks two world records.

(March) Three Mile Island disaster.

Key figures of the decade

Salvador Allende (1908-73)

Marxist physician who was elected President of Chile in 1970 and died in a military coup in 1973.

Yasser Arafat (b.1929)

Palestinian educated in Egypt, who became head of the PLO in 1968. He rejected any idea of a compromise with Israel but was more cautious in his use of terror as a weapon than some of his followers. The PFLP broke away over this issue.

Menachem Begin (b.1913)

Pole who emigrated to Palestine 1942. As a member of the Irgun gang he took part in a guerilla war against the British mandate in Palestine and the UN proposal to give part of Palestine to the Arabs 1943-8. Involved in the blowing up of the King David Hotel in Jerusalem in 1946. Became leader of the Likud Party in 1973 and Prime Minister 1977.

Willi Brandt (b.1913)

German Social Democrat who fled to Norway during the Nazi period. Mayor of West Berlin 1957-66; leader of Social Democratic Party (SPO) 1964-87; Chancellor of West Germany 1970-77. Architect of Ostpolitik and the normalization of relations with East Germany.

Leonid I. Brezhnev (1906-82)

First Secretary of Soviet Communist Party and effective Soviet leader from 1964 until his death. Supporter of Detente abroad but opponent of liberalization at home.

James Callaghan (b.1912)

Labour MP for Cardiff South 1945-1983. Prominent member of the Wilson governments of 1964-70 and 1974-6. Leader of the Labour Party 1976-80; Prime Minister 1976-9. On the right of the Party.

James E. Carter (b.1924)

American Democrat. Governor of Georgia 1971-5. President of the USA 1976-80.

Zhou Enlai (1896-1976)

Founder-member of the Chinese Communist Party (CCP), who took part in the legendary Long March 1934-5. Prime Minister of the Peoples Republic 1949-76 and most cosmopolitan of the Chinese leaders. Close associate of Mao Zedong, on whom he is generally regarded as having had a moderating influence. Probably played a key role in bringing the Cultural Revolution to an end and in restoring links with the USA.

Deng Xiaoping (b.1904)

Leading member of the CCP, who was disgraced during the Cultural Revolution and made a come-back during the 1970s to become the most influential man in China by 1979.

Gerald R. Ford (b.1913)

Republican congressman for Michigan 1948-73. Vice-President of the USA 1973-4. President after the resignation of Nixon 1974-6. Lost the 1976 election to Jimmy Carter.

Germaine Greer (b.1939)

Australian academic and lecturer in English literature at Warwick University, who became one of the best-known and articulate spokes-women for Women's Liberation. Author of *The Female Eunuch* (1971) and *Sex and Destiny: the Politics of Human Fertility* (1984).

Robert Haldeman (b.1926)

Advertising executive who was a close associate of Nixon since 1956. Campaign manager 1968. White House Chief of Staff 1969-73; controlled access to the President. Resigned April 1973 when implicated in Watergate cover-up.

Edward Heath (b.1916)

MP for Bexley since 1950; elected leader of the British Conservative Party in 1965; Prime Minister 1970-4. A life-long pro-European, he led Britain into the EEC, but did not fulfil his promise to curb the unions or bring down inflation. Lost the election of February 1974 to Labour and the leadership contest of 1975 to Margaret Thatcher.

King Hussein (b.1935)

King of Jordan since 1952. Took part in Six Day War in 1967 against Israel, in which he lost the West Bank territories. Until Sadat's reconciliation with Israel he was the most moderate of the Arab leaders and favoured a compromise with Israel. In 1970 he fought a bitter civil war with Palestinian refugees on his territory. Kept Jordan out of the 1973 war.

Ayatollah Ruhollah Khomeini (b.1900)

Iranian Muslim religious leader and bitter critic of the Shah, who returned from exile after the revolution of January 1979 to set up an Islamic Republic.

Henry Kissinger (b.1923)

A refugee from Hitler's Germany who became Professor of Government at Harvard and a well-known writer on early nineteenth-century European diplomacy. Became Nixon's foreign policy adviser in 1969 and Secretary of State (Foreign Minister) 1973-76.

Key figures of the decade

Mao Zedong (1893-1976)

Founder-member of the CCP and its leader during the struggle for power 1927-49. Chairman of Party 1949-76 and most influential figure in China.

Golda Meir (1898-1978)

Born into a Jewish family in Russia, she emigrated to the USA as a child and then to Palestine in 1939. Member of the Labour Party and active in politics since the foundation of the Israeli state. Prime Minister 1969-75.

Robert Mugabe (b.1924)

Marxist and leader of the Zimbabwe African National Union (ZANU). An opponent of any compromise with the principle of majority rule in Southern Rhodesia, he waged a guerilla war against the all-white government of Ian Smith in the 1970s. In 1980, Mugabe became Prime Minister of independent Zimbabwe. Since then he has succeeded in holding the country together in the face of tribal rivalries and white discontent.

Richard M. Nixon (b.1913)

A lawyer who made his name as a fervent anti-communist in the McCarthy era 1950-4; Republican Vice-President 1952-60. He lost the 1960 election to John F. Kennedy and made a come-back in 1968 when he was elected President at the height of the Vietnam protests. He resigned in 1974 as a result of the Watergate scandal, which ruined his reputation.

General Augusto Pinochet (b.1915)

Career officer in the Chilean army, who led coup against President Allende in 1973. Took supreme power in 1974 and suppressed all opposition. Since then, allegations that tens of thousands are detained without trial and that torture is used in prisons have regularly filtered out.

Anwar el Sadat (1918-81)

Egyptian army officer who took part in the military coup that overthrew King Farouk in 1952. Close associate of President Nasser 1954-70 and Vice-President 1969-70. Became President on Nasser's death 1970 and led his country into 1973 Yom Kippur war. Initiated the reconciliation with Israel in 1977, which earned him the reputation of a world statesman but the hatred of many other Arab leaders. Assassinated by a Muslim fanatic in 1981.

Shah of Iran (1919-80)

Mohammed Reza Pahlavi, autocratic ruler of Iran since 1941. His attempts to modernize and westernize the country bought him the emnity of the Muslim clergy. An ally of the United States. His overthrow in 1979 brought an Islamic regime under the Ayatollah Khomeini to power.

Ian Smith (b.1919)

Leader of the all-white Rhodesia Front Party and Prime Minister of Southern Rhodesia (now Zimbabwe) 1962-79. His opposition to majority rule led him to declare independence unilaterally from Britain in 1965 (UDI), a situation that continued until the Lancaster House conference worked out a formula for majority rule in 1979.

Dr Mario Soares (b.1924)

Portuguese Social Democrat and long-time opponent of the dictatorship of Dr Salazar (1932-70) and Dr Caetano (1970-4). Served long periods in prison or in exile 1945-74. Returned after revolution of 1974, and after the outmanoeuvring of the Communists became Prime Minister from 1976-8 and again 1983-5. Elected as President of Portugal 1986.

Alexander Solzhenitsyn (b.1918)

Russian writer who spent eight years in labour camps for unspecified political crimes during the Stalin era. Came to world attention in 1962 when his short story about life in a labour camp, *One Day in the Life of Ivan Denisovitch*, was published in the Soviet Union during the short-lived liberalization of 1960-2. Expelled from the Soviet Union in 1974.

Gloria Steinem (b.1936)

American journalist, grand-daughter of a suffragette. Active in moderate Women's Liberation organizations such as NOW (National Organization of Women) and the Women's Political Caucus. Creator of *Ms.* magazine in 1972.

Margaret Thatcher (b.1925)

Research chemist and tax lawyer by profession; Conservative MP for Finchley since 1959. She came to prominence as Secretary of State for Education in the Heath government 1970-4. Elected as party leader in 1975, she quickly put her stamp on the Tories and led them to victory in the 1979 election.

Karol Wojtyla (b.1920)

Polish Cardinal who was elected Pope under the name of John Paul II in 1978. A cultured man of great intellect, he has made a great impact on Catholics and non-Catholics alike with his unusual zest for life and ability to get close to people.

Sheikh Ahmed Zaki Yamani (b.1930)

Minister of Petroleum and Mineral Resources in Saudi Arabia since 1962. As Chairman of OPEC in 1973, he presented the Arab case for cutting oil supplies to the West. As well as hatred for Israel, Yamani seems to have been motivated by a genuine fear that oil resources would one day run out and should therefore be rationed.

Books for further reading

Few good histories of the 1970s have been published yet. Here are some interesting and useful books concerned with the people and events of the 1970s. All of them should be available from public libraries.

Carl Bernstein and Bob Woodward, *All the President's Men*, Quartet Books, 1974. The story of the first stages of the Watergate revelations.

R.L. Clutterbuck, *Protest and the Urban Guerilla*, Cassell, 1973

Alistair Cooke, *The Americans*, Letters from America 1969-1976, Penguin, 1980

Charles Freeman, *Terrorism*, Batsford, 1981

Michael Hodges, *Living Through History: The 1970s*, Batsford, 1989

C. Dobson, *Black September: Its short, violent history*, Hale, 1975

Colin Mason, *View from Beijing: An Account of the Chinese People Today*, Penguin, 1977

Antony Parsons, *Pride and Fall; Iran 1974-79*, Cape, 1984. Antony Parsons was British Ambassador in Iran during this period.

Sunday Times Insight Team, *Insight on Portugal*, 1975. The year of the captains.

Mark Stephens, *Three Mile Island*, Junction Books, 1980

Dennis Woods, *Biko*, Penguin, 1979

Acknowledgments

The Author and Publishers would like to thank the following for permission to reproduce illustrations: The Keystone Collection for the back cover and pages 3, 4, 6, 7, 8, 9, 11, 14-22, 24-28, 31, 33, 34, 39, 41, 45, 48, 50, 51, 52, 53, 56, 57, 58, 60, 63, 64; Rex Features for page 5; The BBC Hulton Picture Library for pages 36 and 38 and The Camera Press Ltd for pages 13 and 54.

Index

New York 37
Nixon, Richard 8, 12-13 *passim*, **19**, 21,
  24, 26, 30, **31**, 45, 66, 69
Northern Ireland 3, 14, 20, 32, 66
nuclear power 35, 44, 58, 65, 67

Oh! Calcutta 10, 66
oil
  Arab embargo on, *see* energy crisis
  North sea 11, 38, **41**, 53, 57
Olympic Games
  1972 **21**, 22, 66
  1976 46, 67
OPEC (Organization of Petroleum
  Exporting Countries) 25
Ostpolitik 9, **19**
Owen, Dr David **51**

Packer, Kerry 52
Pakistan, civil war in 15, 66
Palestinians
  as refugees 3, 6-7, 38
  terrorist activities of, *see* terrorism
Penatagon Papers 15, 30, 66
Peron, Isabel 26, 33, 44
Peron, Juan 26, 33
ping-pong diplomacy 12
Pinochet, General Augusto 26, 69
pop music 4-5, 10, 22, 46, 52, 64
Pope John Paul II **56**, 62, 69
Portugal, 3, 9, **32**, 38, 44, 66, 67
Presley, Elvis 52, 67
punk rock 4, **52**, 67

Rahman, Sheikh Mujibur 15, 21, 39, 67
Reagan, Ronald 5, 62
recession 4, 36-7
Red Rum 40
Rindt, Jochen 10, 66
Rotten, Johnny **5**, 52
rugby union 46, 58

Sadat, Anwar el 9, 48-9 *passim*, 56, 67, 69

Salazar, Dr 9, 33
SALT (Strategic Arms Limitation Treaty)
  I 18, **19**, 66
  II 56
Sampson, Nikos 32
Saturday Night Fever 58
Schleyer, Hans-Martin 50
Seveso disaster 44, **45**, 67
Sex Pistols 5, **52**, 67
Silver Jubilee **51**
smallpox, elimination of 58, 67
Smith, Ian 43, 62, 69
Soares, Mario 33, 69
social changes 4, 5
Solzhenitsyn, Alexander 10, **34**, 69
Somoza, General 62
South Africa
  and international sport 10, 40
  intervention in Angola 42-3 *passim*
  TV in 40
  unrest in 42-3, **50**, 67
Southern Rhodesia *see* Zimbabwe
Soviet Union 10, 12, 42-3 *passim*;
  see also detente, Afghanistan
Soyuz II deaths 17, 66
space exploration
  manned flights 11, 16, 23, 41
  unmanned planetary exploration 29, 35, 47
  space shuttle 41, 53, 65
  space stations 17
  US-Soviet co-operation 41, 67
  see also Apollo 13
Spain 3, 39, 44
Star Wars 52
Steinem, Gloria 16, 69
Stoppard, Tom 34
Sydney Opera house **28**, 66
Syria 24

Taiwan 12, 13, 55
Tate Gallery 46
technology
  advances in 4, 16, 59, 65

loss of faith in 4, 5, 65
television 28, 40, 52, 64
tennis 16, 28, 34, 40, 46, 52, 58, **64**, 66
terrorism 3
  in Canada 9
  in Germany 3, 21, 50, 67
  in Italy 3, **56**, 67
  in Northern Ireland 3 *see also* IRA
  in the air 6-7, 21, 50, 66, 67
  by Palestinian groups, 6-7, 20, 24, 50, 66, 67
test tube baby 3, 59, 67
Thatcher, Margaret 5, 39, 57, **63**, 67, 69
theatre 46
  new plays in 5, 16, 34, 63
  end of censorship in 5, 10
Thorpe, Jeremy 45, 57
Three-day week **27**, 66
Three Mile Island 65, 67
Times The, suspension of 57, 67
Trident 23
Tutankhamun exhibition 22, 66

UNITA *see* Angola
United Nations 12, 24
United States of America 3, 8, 15, 42-3 *passim*
  44, 62; *see also* Vietnam, Cambodia, China
  detente, Watergate

Vietnam
  refugees from 56
  war in 3, 19, **26**, **38**, 66, 67

Watergate 21, 26, 30, **31**
Winter of Discontent **63**
Wilson, Harold 32, 45, 67
Women in Love 10
Women's Liberation 3, 5, **9**, 15, 16

Yamani, Sheikh Ahmed Zaki 25, 69
Yom Kippur War **24**-5, 66

Zhou Enlai 12, 46, 68
Zimbabwe 3, 43, 62, 67